Early Adolescent
ART EDUCATION

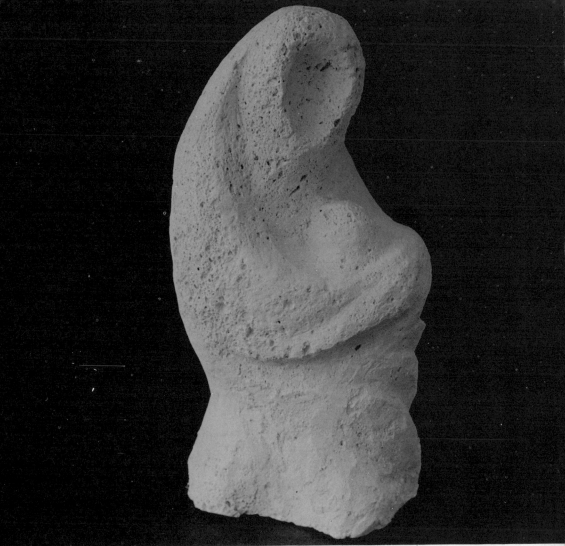

A sensitive interpretation in plaster of the
human figure and motherhood, by a young girl.

A NOTE ABOUT THE AUTHOR

Carl Reed was educated at Pratt Institute and New York University.
His career includes positions as instructor in commercial art, Pratt
Institute; lecturer at the U. S. Military Academy, West Point; art
director, M. Lowell advertising agency; illustrator for magazines
and men's fashions; fine art exhibitor; member of the New York
state education department art consultant committee; supervisor of
art, Montclair Academy and the Nyack, N. Y., public schools; and,
at present, associate art supervisor, New York state. During the
school year 1954-55, he toured the United States under a Ford
Fellowship grant. His work proves him to be one of the brilliant
younger leaders in American education.

Early Adolescent

ART EDUCATION

Carl Reed

Associate Art Supervisor
New York State Department of Education

Chas. A. Bennett Co., Inc.
Peoria, Illinois

Library of Congress Catalog Card Number: 57-5430

PRINTED BY PHOTO-OFFSET IN THE UNITED STATES OF AMERICA

ACKNOWLEDGMENTS

As MAN is the incarnation of his experiences, he must humbly acknowledge his associates, friends, teachers, and students who have affected his thinking which results in his productivity.

Indebtedness is due to the several State Art Supervisors who generously gave of their time to discuss art education, and their programs and philosophies—Alice Baumgarner of New Hampshire, Sara Joyner and Richard Wiggin of Virginia, George Miller of Pennsylvania, Edith Mitchell of Delaware— and especially Mary Godfrey of Virginia and C. D. Gaitskell of Ontario, who provided stimulating, informative discussions, fine food and transportation throughout their areas.

My first art teacher—Miss Minnie Bates—and my mother, through their understanding and encouragement, were most influential in my choosing art education as a career. Mr. Vincent Popolizio, the New York State Supervisor of Art, advocated my writing on art education for the junior high level. Dr. Jack Arends of Teachers College advised me in setting the tone and direction of this manuscript. Paul Van Winkle's faith has been encouraging and his suggestions have improved the clarity of many sections.

Grateful acknowledgment is due to the Ford Foundation for the Advancement of Education which sponsored a year of travel throughout America; also to Mr. Leonard Miller and to Mr. George Grice, who have contributed articles for the manuscript.

5

I am further indebted to: Mr. Milton Immermann who spent considerable time with me and supplied several industrial design illustrations; Mr. Edward Rannells of the University of Kentucky, who kindly loaned me his copy of the out-of-print bulletin "Art Education in the Junior High School" for reference and granted permission to quote from it; Dr. Harry Wood of Arizona State College, who arranged for me to conduct a graduate seminar in art education, and to the many Arizona students of that seminar who discussed each chapter of the manuscript with me; the professional artists who have permitted reproduction of their works and the many teachers who have supplied the works of young student artists for illustrations; the publishers who have granted permission to quote from their publications; the numerous city art supervisors and department heads who gave their time to me for discussion; the many one room school teachers all over America who accepted my unannounced intrusion; Superintendent K. R. MacCalman, who lent understanding support to my efforts and experiments to develop an effective art program in the Nyack schools.

I am deeply grateful to my ever-understanding wife who postponed many meals, supplied refreshments in the wee hours of the mornings, and was always willing to proofread, listen to newly written sections, and to comment on them as a self-named "average art teacher."

I am mindful and grateful for the continued blessings of the Divine Providence which arranges through a complexity of circumstances the opportunities for us to create and to exchange our ideas.

C.L.R.

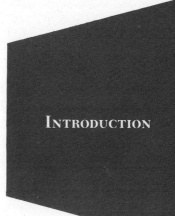

INTRODUCTION

THIS book emphasizes the value of art in the curriculum for the junior high level and stresses the importance of understanding the young adolescent in order to effect a successful art program. It explores an attainable set of aims and objectives, in order to assist the art teacher in defining his program, and to provide the administrator with the information necessary for him to give wider support to the emphasis on art education.

A planned program is suggested here, peculiarly adapted for *the most important phase of art education—that for the young adolescent*—which previously has been most seriously neglected.

Today finds art education in America established as an important, definite factor in child development, and in a uniquely advantageous position to make tremendous advances in areas which it has failed to emphasize.

The receding influence of "progressive education" has left in its wake many art teachers seeking guidance and direction. The more traditionally trained teacher has felt the need for information on current trends in creative art.

There is increased emphasis on the value of participation in art for emotional release and psychiatric therapy. This makes it essential that the art teacher be well enough informed on this particular stress and approach to be able to view them in their proper relation to our primary objectives, functions, and limitations in the art program.

The conflict between the "progressive" and the "traditional" approaches to art education has to be resolved, and a positive and unified line of action adopted, if the art program is to be universally accepted, make advancement, and provide a significant contribution to education and child development.

The current unprecedented popular interest in art provides ideal circumstances for art educators to gain broader acceptance of the values of art education in the secondary curriculum, just as they have been in the elementary schools.

The trend toward more and more junior high schools has continued, but the development of a suitable program of art for the junior high student has not kept pace with it. Among the notably few art educators who have given consideration to the art program for this level there is a wide spread of thinking. Most school systems have not felt it necessary to present an art course specially adapted to the young adolescent. And so there is an unfortunate lack of organized opinion regarding art education on this level!

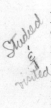

To make possible the presentation of current, valid, and pertinent material related to an effective program of art education, the author spent a full year seeing at first hand what is actually going on in the schools of America. The investigation covered hundreds of public and private schools—schools in wealthy suburban areas, schools in industrial cities, Indian reservation schools, schools supported by industrial organizations, small rural schools, large urban schools, schools in the mountains, schools in the deserts, schools for children of transient farm laborers, schools on the west coast and east coast, schools in the north and south. Visits were made to teacher training colleges, commercial art studios, fine art studios, and professional art schools. The question of the best program of art for the young adolescent was discussed in detail with junior high art teachers, city art directors, college art teachers, commercial artists, fine artists, guidance counselors, state directors of school art, school administrators, and parents.

This vital contact with the pulse of American art education as evaluated in the light of many years of teaching art on the junior high level has resulted in the philosophy of art education, ideas, and suggestions presented here.

TABLE OF CONTENTS

Being an art teacher on the junior high level presents a
stimulating challenge. It is the broadest, and probably most
important job for art educators. With a thorough understanding of the young adolescent, a solidly developed program and
a willingness to pick up the gauntlet of these teenagers, you can
enjoy the satisfying thrill of accomplishment in one of the most
exciting areas of art education.

Art programs in America

By visiting hundreds of American schools and by studying
the syllabi of scores of others we find that the art programs
currently run the gamut from the most formal and regimented
type of unimaginative sequence of projects to the other extreme of a most laissez-faire type of undirected activities. In
the first case a planned course of activities called "art" is offered,
which takes the student through a step-by-step sequence of
drawings—and sometimes paintings—in a completely two-dimensional experience. Imagination and creative self-expression are ignored. At the other extreme we find a situation in
which art is offered primarily as a means of emotional release
through a series of manipulative expressions—with little or no
teaching involved. In this latter instance the role of the teacher
is reduced to that of the person who supplies art materials and
provides an "emotionally charged background." Somewhere
in this vast spread of planning (or lack of planning) there is
an educationally justifiable program of art which should be effectively organized and developed.

11

Contributions of progressive education

Fortunately the influence of progressive education increased interest in art in the curriculum and freed many art teachers from narrow methods and hackneyed offerings. Creativity was stressed, *but* techniques and learning were often neglected. A vastly more interesting and exciting program was evolved; *however*, some of the activity was of questionable educational worth.

It is obvious that the educational pendulum is now swinging back from its most "progressive" point. We must be alert so that improper leadership does not successfully encourage the completion of the swing back to its most traditional point. Though it will be readily granted that the traditional art training of the past embodied many elements which have a place in our current art program, there were also many deficiencies!

The peremptory obligation of the art teacher now is to seek out the best of both periods and to blend it into a vital art program suited to the needs of the student. This should be done without the loss of any of the gains of the most recent years and with the inclusion of that which is worthy from the previous more traditional period.

Teacher training in the traditional manner

Many teachers, whose formal training as art educators took place several years ago, were trained in a factual, realistic manner, from early childhood, primarily in drawing. The area of "expressionism" wasn't even mentioned, if their instructors knew that it existed. Knowledge and use of three-dimensional materials in art productions were entirely overlooked, except in crafts. The training in art was directed almost from the very beginning toward the developing of *a few artists*. Lack of direct contact with the contemporary materials, methods, and objectives has caused teachers thus trained to be reluctant to extend themselves into new areas, and in many cases has made them antagonistic—in self-defense. They have been afraid of the newer art education because of its stress on creative expression with unfamiliar materials and tools. Now they are further confused by a school of thought which presents art as a psychiatric therapy.

12

Many of these teachers are imbued with a real love of art and art teaching, and humanity. If you are one of them, an *open-minded approach* to a study of newer art attitudes, methods, and materials will prove interesting and rewarding. (1) Visit classes of outstanding teachers in experimental schools. (2) See and analyze some of the magnificent shows of modern sculpture and painting. (3) Attend state, regional, or national art education association meetings. (4) Restudy the use of display in the better magazines. (5) Reinvestigate the aims of contemporary artists. (6) Observe the current productions of industrial designers. (7) Be constantly alert for ideas which can be adapted to your program. You will find that it is inspiring to become a part of a growing movement, and lots more fun, as you come to enjoy the challenge of creativity as it is conceived by contemporary artists, using modern materials. Your background of teaching experience and your knowledge of art, coupled with your new interests, are sure to make your life more exciting and your teaching contributions more satisfying and effective.

The more recent training of teachers

Our younger teachers have been guided in the more progressive approach and have the advantage of a freer and more exploratory use of materials. However, many of them have missed the training which enables one to understand the young adolescent who (1) desires to work realistically, or who (2) demands assistance in learning techniques which will help him express himself more easily. Some more recently trained teachers have been led to believe that young adolescents should instinctively create, when provided with materials and/or an emotional stimulus. They are unable to help the student who needs more than this. Also they fail to appreciate the student who rejects large, quickly rendered, loose painting and gains most personal satisfaction and growth from minute linear representations of his environment, or commercial designing. The boy who shuns watercolors and finds his satisfaction in lettering, or in tight renderings of airplanes, refrigerators, or "hot rods," also has been a problem to this teacher, who has not been sensitized to anything but an emotional type of artwork.

13

Many younger teachers have not yet discovered that effective art appreciation, which is a primary aim of art education, requires a sound knowledge and understanding of all art forms. Free, undirected expression alone in art materials will not bring about true understanding or appreciation.

The aim of this book is to help the new teacher to make a more understanding, effective, and graceful entrance into the art program on the junior high school level; to help the active traditional teacher orient himself in contemporary art education, in the light of his past training and art concepts.

The successful art teacher must constantly re-evaluate his teaching in the light of his background and the current trends and information on art education. He must discard that which he finds has no value or that which has been maintained primarily for expediency or for fear of the unknown; he must *constantly revitalize* valuable elements of the old, incorporate the best of the new, and redefine his aims, methods, and objectives.

This is a concept that has been gravely neglected in modern art education.

Art as a challenge

The average child in a normal situation will be able to meet the challenge of any ordinary art problem as he does other problems in life. An art program bereft of all challenge will be of little value educationally, mentally, or emotionally to the normal child. The recent psychotherapeutic stress on art has caused many art teachers to "bleed" their programs of all educational challenge for fear of the grave possibilities of provoking "shock," "frustration," and "crisis."

We can safely assume that most of our students in schools are near average, normal, healthy children. We should approach them as such. The art teacher who considers each child as a psychiatric problem, and attempts to interpret the inner soul, or to discover mental and emotional problems through the art productions, may be treading on very dangerous ground and entirely missing his objective. That art may be used as a therapy is one more of its attributes, but the aim of art education is not therapy, nor is it a means of separating the rational from the irrational. Though psychiatrists may

14

use art expression as one means of psychoanalysis, *this is not the mission of art education.*

Art in individual development

Art education has a positive value in the general education program. It offers unique developmental factors which no other subject possesses, and it educates for a tremendous personal enrichment.

Yet art has had a real struggle to secure for itself the place it deserves in the child education program. Science and vocational training have had financial aid and general encouragement from industry and government. Art has had to depend on individuals alone. Hence it has been difficult to present administrators with concerted evidence that justifies emphasis on art in the secondary school program. Community pressures have also emphasized stress on academic, scientific, and vocational subjects rather than on art education. Consequently, art has been more or less tolerated on the secondary level and stressed mainly on a vocational basis.

Definition of "junior high school"

Until recently the 8-4 division—eight years of elementary grades and four years of high school—has been most employed. The advent of the junior high school produced a 6-3-3 division —six years of elementary school, three years of junior high school, and three years of senior high school. (Many communities, especially smaller ones, have adopted a 6-6 program for economy.) The much less prevalent 6-4-4 division provides a four-year junior high school between a six-year elementary school and a four-year senior high school and junior college combination.

Regardless of the type of grade division in which the young adolescent is involved *he must*—in order to be reached effectively—*be offered a program which considers his natural developmental period*, with its unique interests, abilities, drives, attitudes, and objectives. The material presented here aims to assist the teacher in understanding the inter-related characteristics of this puberal phase, and the aims, content, and methods of current, successful trends in art education on this level.

15

Course adjustment for the young adolescent

The art course which aims at attracting young teenagers must provide activities which are interesting, educational, and challenging. Activities must be arranged which (1) appeal to maturing students who now for the first time are feeling the magnetic attraction of dates, "hot rods," lipstick, evening gowns, athletic teams, and "hit parades." (2) Projects which challenge the rapidly developing critical and manual skills must be included. (3) To make art come alive, activities must be intertwined with everyday living. (4) The student's world must include the creations of contemporary artists who directly affect our lives and thinking—the works of illustrators, industrial and textile designers, advertising artists, interior decorators, architects, and cartoonists, as well as the works of the fine artists of the past and present.

Weakness of the 8-4 program

Rarely does a course of study stress the importance of a course adjustment in art to meet the demands of the young adolescent. Too often the 8-4 program presupposes the student to be a child until he reaches the ninth grade. In this type of grade division the art program of the 7th and 8th grade is usually only an extension of the art activities of the intermediate grades. Then suddenly at the end of the 8th grade, without any transitory period, the student is treated as a full fledged adolescent, and is expected to be able to cope with a more mature type of pedagogy as it is employed in the high school educational organization.

For the majority of our American students no provision is made for the continuation of art education after the elementary grades. In addition many art programs are based on the assumption that the natural desire for creative expression of the young child carries over into adolescence, regardless of what type of art program is offered during the junior high years. As we know, this is not the case.

We re-emphasize here that the art program for the young adolescent must be a unique one, especially adjusted for him, regardless of what type of division is used for the various grade groupings.

16

Adult interest in creativity

During the past years we, as art educators, may have felt that we were doing a very satisfactory job with school children in stimulating interest in art and in encouraging participation in creativity. Very few students seemed to carry over art interests into adult life. Yet suddenly we discovered that when someone started selling "by-the-numbers" paint sets, hundreds of thousands of adults were interested enough to spend millions of dollars yearly on such equipment. The entrepreneurs promoting the sale of paint sets did something which art educators failed to do—they caused thousands of people to become interested in painting, though these same people had appeared to lack interest. We have been inclined to be critical of "numbers" promoters but we must acknowledge their shrewdness. Let us "pick up the ball" from there.

Junior high art course is terminal

In considering the development of the most effective art program for the junior high level, remember that for most students this is a terminal course. Most schools do not require the pursuit of an art course after the eighth or ninth grade. And, of course, most students do not elect one even if it is available. This then is the last opportunity for most of our future citizens to have any contact with an organized art experience. The art attitude which the student will carry through life will be materially affected, if not completely formulated, during these junior high years.

This places an awesome responsibility on the planners of the art activities for young teenagers. Unless the student becomes actively involved in a stimulating art process at this time, he will probably leave school with a strong antipathy for art, or with the concept that art is a play activity for the elementary child with little or no relationship to adult living.

The vital importance of a terminal art course presents a very real challenge to the junior high school art teacher and administrator.

17

CHAPTER II   AIMS AND OBJECTIVES

THE END product of a total educational exposure should
be a well integrated and cultured personality. Art has a very
definite contribution to make in the development of this desired type of person.

The vital and exciting art program will have well established aims and objectives. Both the instructor and the students will know what these are and how each problem—and
parts of problems—relates to the overall program.

To establish art solidly in the school curriculum, the administrator rightfully wants assurance that positive, worthwhile,
attainable educational objectives are set up by the art department.

The art teacher must constantly re-appraise his course in
terms of his aims and objectives. All problems must be an integral part of his plan. This does not mean that confining
limitations are placed on the breadth or scope of art activities.
It means that a check is made constantly to be sure that the
art activities are of purposeful educational value.

Students appreciate knowing what their goals are; they
enjoy the evaluation of their work when they have reached that
goal. It is through this process that growth takes place in all
education, including art education.

Do not be overly ambitious with what you expect art education to accomplish. *It is within the areas where art can contribute most* that we should place our emphasis!

Moholy-Nagy described art as an essential balance gauge.
"Even in its seeming isolation, the experience of art as the

18

thermometer of necessities is indispensable for society. The true function of art is to be the graph of our time, an intuitive search for the missing equilibrium among our emotional, intellectual, and social lives. Art is the most intimate language of the senses, a direct linking of man to man."[1]

The following aims have been established over a period of years. They have proved satisfactory when used with students at the young teen-age level. They serve as a criterion in judging projects for the junior high art program. Each problem should be planned and developed so as to serve directly several aims. No one aim should be set up in isolation from all of the others.

AIMS

1. To develop a sensitivity to and appreciation of art.

2. To provide opportunities for creative expression.

3. To teach the fundamentals and techniques which will provide the means of achieving art expression.

4. To develop satisfying avocational interests.

5. To seek out the talented and to provide counseling in the choosing of a vocation.

6. To provide a gradual transition from pre-adolescent art training to art education suiting the needs and interests of adolescents.

7. To provide for social experiences and an opportunity to engage in wholesome activities with the opposite sex.

8. To correlate art with other areas of the curriculum.

9. To develop the relationship between contemporary art and daily living.

10. To help in the development of well-integrated personalities. ·

The purpose of the course in art must be constantly in the mind of the art teacher. The instructor who is conducting a program with such broad and indefinite objectives that he can not always connect the classroom activity with several in a set of specific aims, is probably not producing educationally. He is following an uncharted course and is lost in his aimless sea.

Let us consider each of these aims.

1. ART APPRECIATION

To provide for the experiences and the acquisition of knowledge and skills which will develop an understanding and appreciation of man's creative expression is a most important aim of art education. Whole cultures of the past are interpreted through the art expressions which have been preserved or rediscovered.

Today some of us are almost completely surrounded by a physical environment built by man. In large metropolitan areas one has to look to the sky above the walled-in canyons to see a unit of the landscape which has not been made or altered by man. (Even the skies are now being patterned by the vapor trails of invisible jet aircraft.)

In suburban and agricultural areas the contours of our terrain are being reshaped by man. Whole mountains are moved and rebuilt into dams or road beds over valleys. Ribbons of concrete highways cross and crisscross America. The areas adjacent to all of our newer parkways have been landscaped with an eye toward beautification.

All of our interior living and working spaces are designed and decorated by man. We create new designs and adapt those of antiquity. All of our tools, utensils, conveyances, and even our weapons are crafted by designers. Never before has man been so surrounded by productions designed for his convenience, use, and pleasure. The individual who is not sensitized to aesthetics is being cheated because much of his surroundings is without meaning to him. It is as though he walked through his environment shrouded in a fog.

So, without regard to the specific vocational plans of junior high students, all should be provided with art experiences which will assure a richer and fuller appreciation of the creative expression with which they will be surrounded for the rest of their lives. For nearly all students, the junior high program is the last contact they will have with a course of study planned to provide the development of an appreciation of the arts. This places a grave responsibility on the art teacher. If we fail here we produce a mass of artistic illiterates. The following statement was made by William G. Whitford several years ago. It is still true today, although, perhaps, to a slightly lesser degree. "Color specialists, interior decorators, civic beauty commissions and numerous other service agencies are supplying for the present generation what the school failed to, namely, the knowledge necessary for meeting the common art problems of the twentieth century."[2]

Appreciation cannot be taught. Each student has to develop it within himself. The student must identify himself with the subject matter that is to be appreciated. This includes knowing, and to know something one has to learn. Thus *art appreciation concerns itself with what has to be learned.* This requires (1) real analysis and understanding of art principles, (2) knowledge of the limitations and possibilities in the use of materials, (3) the meaning of creativity, and (4) the problems involved in it. Obviously, then, art appreciation cannot be accomplished as an isolated aim or subject area.

As a student completes a piece of artwork, he must compare the relation of the art principles and design elements employed to those same principles and elements as used by other artists in creations of the past and present. This will enable him to sense the kinship between his creative ability and that of all mankind.

Use of standard principles

Point out the principles of arrangement—dominance and subordination, repetition or rhythm, and balance. Show how these are dependent on line, mass, color, and value.

For example, when paper sculpture problems are completed by a group of students, it could be pointed out that the various shapes are emphasized by the tonal values of shadows which are created on the forms. Then show how architects develop accents, balance, and rhythm in creating interesting

21

façades of buildings when only one-color material is used. Note the tonal beauty of certain white Georgian Colonial buildings.

Dress designers are also conscious of values when developing styles in materials of one color. The folding, draping, and pleating are all used to create emphasis in dark and light tones.

Work of industrial designers and sculptors could be profitably shown and discussed here.

The constant repetition of this type of procedure will develop the student's ability to recognize relationships between *familiar* art objects and the principles which apply to them, and other objects which are new to him. This "growing" appreciation will carry on throughout life.

The mere participation in creative expression will not bring about appreciation. There must be *impression* as well as *expression*. When the creations of others make a definite impression, then appreciation takes place. "It is a psychological fact that if they (the students) give themselves over to appreciation, they take into themselves some quality of the thing appreciated, and enlarge their capacity for further appreciation."[3]

"To appreciate art is to value it and need it, and as art becomes necessary to individuals it becomes necessary to society . . . . Thus the primary objective of individual appreciation assumes a social character in art education."[4]

A balance of forces in society is necessary in any culture. Art is necessary to maintain this balance. Unbridled scientific advancement and experimentation without the influence of aesthetics can easily destroy our society.

Limits of appreciation

In an attempt to develop appreciation the teacher must not expect to find student interest in art productions which are beyond their developmental level or interests. We cannot look for junior high students to be able to fully appreciate Pollock, Lipschitz, Calder, or Picasso, or even Michelangelo or Da Vinci.

2. CREATIVE EXPRESSION

There is no question but what the art program should pro-

22

An oil painting showing a sensitive arrangement of forms. Colors are subtle but powerful.

vide for creative expression. This does not mean a laissez-faire situation which allows students to play with materials and demands praise for every nondescript combination of materials and techniques. Dewey wrote that " . . . . what is some-times called an art of self-expression might better be termed one of self-exposure; it discloses character—or lack of character—to others. In itself it is only a spewing forth."[5]

Creative self-expression is an educational process which involves intelligence and emotions. The creative process can be carried on only in an art classroom where students are deeply engrossed in their creations. All too often art teachers use "self-expression" as an excuse for a completely inexcusable classroom situation in which nothing is happening that is edu-cationally justifiable. Creation demands a sincere application of all skills, techniques, emotions, and information which will enable the best possible development of the individual's origi-nal concept of the creation. This sort of educational process cannot go on in a chaotic classroom studio.

Of course one finds an abundance of sheer joy and excitement in a creative studio. But there is much more than that to art education. The student's real enjoyment and gratification come when he knows he has successfully completed a project calling for something extra in applying his knowledge, skill, and imagination.

Playing with wire, clay, or watercolors, for days on end, "to see what will come out of it," is not creative expression, because it is neither creative nor expressive. This point is worth much thought. There is a place for experimentation in the art program. However, when the student begins to feel that he is "playing at art," his junior-high program does not fulfill the aims of a unit of work. Nor does it satisfy the general aims of art education.

One of the most gratifying experiences in art teaching is to enjoy with a student the deep satisfaction which comes from a successful creation, if it has been a real challenge mentally, emotionally, and physically. Such experiences justify the inclusion of an art program in a curriculum set up to develop well rounded individuals!

Meaning of "self-expression"

Self-expression, of course, means that the self is projected into a true expression through whatever medium is used in the creative process. It follows then that each creation will be as different as the student is who creates it. Whenever there are many look-alike solutions, we can be sure there is little or no self-expression. The superior art teacher will be always striving to stimulate personal interpretations of each project.

All students should be able to participate *expressively* in a creative art program. This does not mean that every student can be an artist. That would trivialize art. However, all students can be given opportunities to enjoy the thrill of creativity.

This whole area is explored in more detail in the chapter on the "Creative Approach."

3. FUNDAMENTALS AND TECHNIQUES

There are techniques and skills of expression, fundamentals and principles, to be learned in the art area, just as in

24

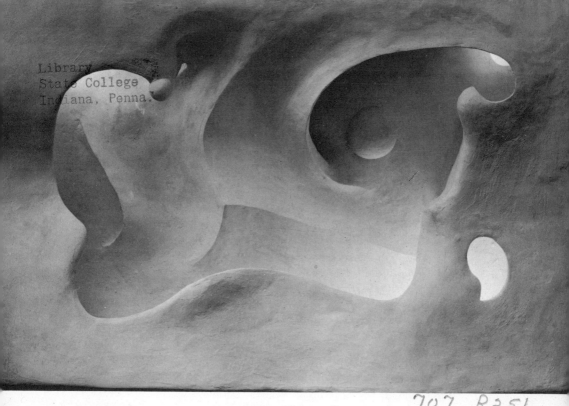

NYACK JR.-SR. HIGH SCHOOL, NYACK, N. Y.

Experiences in creating three-dimensional art forms such as this original plaster wall sculpture are an important part of the art program. Below: Wood and screen frame for the wall sculpture. Wiring and bulbs are installed.

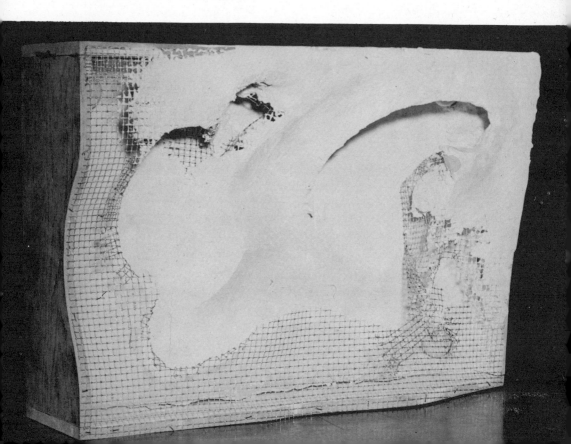

other subject matter areas. There are things to study, to learn, and to know. The critical aesthetic judgment of the student will mature as he learns about art. His ability to create will be broadened as he gains a facility with various techniques of expression. Techniques, of course, are not taught as ends in themselves. But they have to be taught if they are to be learned. They are necessary to make possible creative expression on a more mature level than the child has been producing in the primary and intermediate grades. Too often, when teachers are asked about techniques, they give the stock answer that "techniques are taught as the need arises." *Be sure to recognize the arisen need!* Whenever the student is struggling to create with an unfamiliar material or with an advanced effect, he probably can be helped by instruction in a special technique. This does not mean dictating his method, but merely to advise him concerning those steps which might facilitate his construction. If this is not true, the teacher's years of experience, experimentation, knowledge, and training are of no value. The actions and statements of some art educators represent the art teacher as having no function beyond supplying the materials and providing stimulation. Thus one might conclude that a satisfactory art teaching job could be done by any stimulating personality.

The fact is, art learning needs *art teaching!*

4. AVOCATIONAL INTERESTS

Art as a hobby is reaching a peak of popularity that can be expected in our maturing nation. The great movement toward national expression in design and the wider use of materials has proved stimulating. Introducing problems with a variety of materials in the classroom will create an interest in them which may be developed later into a hobby. Many such hobbies can be turned into considerable profit.

Some students will have already developed hobbies in the art area which they will want to carry on in the art studio. This provides an opportunity for the teacher to help broaden the student's scope and encourage the application of principles which will guide him toward more successful results. Then the art curriculum becomes a living program. For in-

26

stance, many girls will in later years use their knowledge of color and design in home decoration, dress planning and selection, and community improvement. Many students will use their experiences with clay and other materials to develop a worthwhile leisuretime activity. Many of the hobbies begun in junior high art classes will serve to enrich the leisure hours of the adult.

5. Vocational counseling

The junior high student is becoming aware of his approaching independence from his family. Boys and girls both will shortly be considering the responsibilities of marriage and a family. Most will have to choose a vocation that will make them economically independent. They should be able to look to the art teacher for counseling—especially those who have developed an interest in art as a vocation.

Some students with exceptional talent in art will not have thought of art as a career. The teacher should be alert to point out opportunities in the art field to these students.

This subject is more thoroughly developed in the chapter on "Counseling."

6. Articulation

The course in junior high art cannot be adequately developed as a separate unit unconnected with the senior high school or, especially, the elementary grades. The art attitude brought up from the elementary classes is of the utmost importance. There must be a very positive working relationship between the elementary and junior high teachers. Unless the student leaves the elementary course with an assurance that art is a pleasant, satisfying experience in which he himself can successfully participate, the junior high art teacher faces an almost impossible task. The integration of art on these two levels is too often neglected.

It is not the intention of this book to explore the elementary program of art. However, the elementary program should provide for the interest of some of the upper intermediate grade students who have begun to mature more rapidly than their classmates. Otherwise, they will become disinterested, if not antagonistic. These students carry over into the junior high art classes an attitude which impairs their success and the success of the art program.

Furthermore, with a vital, exciting elementary and junior high background, the number of students who elect senior high courses will be increased. Many adjustments can be made in the junior high to provide for students who are planning to continue art as a preparation for a vocation, or for broadening of their life program.

7. SOCIAL EXPERIENCES

The junior high student needs opportunities to engage in activities with classmates of both sexes. Many boys and girls become very shy, and as a result associate closely only with their own sex.

The relaxed, informal organization of the art class provides a good atmosphere for pleasant social intercourse which is so essential in this period of maturation. Most other subjects in the average junior high curriculum are not as able to provide the "mixing action" which is present in the well-conducted art studio. (1) The successful art creation tends to help *establish the respect* of classmates of both sexes. This is especially welcomed by girls. (2) Co-operation within a group is developed by sharing tools and equipment, and by working together in the same medium or on the same group project. (3) Working together on art projects develops leadership as well as the ability to be cooperative followers.

8. CORRELATION

Art is a "natural" for integration with other subjects in the curriculum. Perhaps its ease of integration is a disadvantage! The correlation with limited-aim subjects often permits them to invade and adopt art for their own uses to the point that the subject of art loses identity and curricular importance. Art has a very definite contribution of its own to make and this fact should not be subordinated or forgotten for the sake of integration.

28

Many school groups are working on the further integration of subjects. This is called by various names—core, common learnings, general education, unified studies, homeroom-centered curriculum, unified learnings. All indicate an effort to provide a curriculum which tends to meet the needs, interest, and problems of youth as adequately and effectively as possible. While some success has come from this effort, many school systems have given it up for a bad job. To be successful, this type of program requires a very well-trained staff and excellent leadership.

If it dominates the thinking of a group, the cause of art is advanced by adopting the core program. If not, the art program loses ground to other dominating subjects.

Regarding integration, Winslow writes: "Art should be integrated in the curriculum with whatever it is integrated with in life. Therefore the curriculum cannot afford to be anything short of life itself, in which all areas contribute to effective living. The amount of integration of art and social studies should, for example, be about the same in school as in life."[6]

Securing a place for art

The art teacher will do well to maintain close liaison with other instructors in the junior high curriculum in order to take advantage of opportunities in the integrated course. This will tend to interest other teachers in the art program and promote your field in the eyes of students and parents. A student who has been interested only in the sciences will accept art instruction when, for instance, he finds he can make a mobile using the universe as a theme. One whole art section became intensely interested in a project in structural representation as a result of a problem in mathematics which called for the making of freehand drawings.

9. CONTEMPORARY ART IN DAILY LIVING

The activities of the art program must lead to appreciation and understanding of contemporary art, as it is involved in the students' daily life.

29

Too often art appreciation has been concerned largely with the paintings of the old masters. Not only the paintings of our time, but modern man's creative cultural statement—that of the industrial designer—have been overlooked almost completely. Much of our environment is shaped by the industrial designer. Whole cities and countrysides are shaped by artists. Many people decry the fact that our material culture is so lacking in aesthetics. They lament the lack of support of art. These people fail to state that there are more *products* aesthetically designed in our world than ever before. *Almost nothing is produced today that has not been styled.*

"Beauty, for a long time truant, is returning to the common rounds of daily life: we encounter a new and thrilling man-made beauty on our highways and parked at our curbstones; it flies in the air above us and spans in graceful webs our rivers and our bays: occasionally it rises high and serene in our cities, and in long winding ribbons of parkway it penetrates the country. Some fortunate men work in the midst of beauty in our factories and workshops, pioneers in a new concept of labor, and beauty is bought again in shops that sell only useful things. It enters our homes and takes up its abode in our kitchens, our bathrooms and our cellars, the first essays toward a frame of beauty for our routine hours."

There should be a direct relationship between teaching the principles of design and color, and the application by students to their solutions of everyday art problems in contemporary living. The knowledge and skills and attitudes gained in the art classes should assist these students in creating for themselves a more graceful and pleasant living environment.

10. INTEGRATION OF PERSONALITY

Participation in the creative art program contributes materially to successful interaction of the personality with its environment. A balance of intellect and emotion is essential in the well-integrated individual. Rosabell MacDonald states: "There is a balance between his receiving and giving, his contemplation and action, his concentration and relaxation, and his individual and social living. A man developed on both appreciative and creative side is a man with a chance of remaining whole and balanced . . . . A man cannot live by bread alone; so also he cannot live by acquisition and exterior values alone. To feel that he is actually a part of life, he must live sensually and emotionally as well as rationally."[8]

The student who successfully creates finds great security in this ability. Building creative faith within the individual is of no small importance in our indecisive world.

Davidson makes a statement about painting which is equally true of all creative art processes: "The painter is his own judge of facts, his eyes are his authority. Only his own decision determines what he does with his brush. And so he unconsciously cultivates the habit of independence and reliance upon his own mind and sense responses."[9]

"A human being is developed by the crystallization of the whole of his experience. Our present system of education contradicts this axiom by emphasizing single fields of activity.

"Instead of extending our realm of action, as primitive man was forced to do, since he combined in one person, hunter, craftsman, builder, and physician, we concern ourselves with a single specific vocation, leaving other capacities unused."[10] The broad concepts of the creative art program tends to alleviate this stress on specialization in education.

Successful participation in the art program can be used to help a gifted student adjust to his entire school life. An example of this was a talented junior high boy, who was having a disastrous time in his whole 7th grade program. The art teacher, who recognized his ability and knew him as an outstanding and co-operative student, was surprised to find child study conference reports indicating a definite conflict. The art teacher suggested a change in his schedule which would increase his time in the art studio. Though this undeserved "rewarding" was frowned upon by some of his teachers, it soon began to show favorable results. The art teacher worked patiently with the boy, discussed his future plans with him, his chances of success in the commercial art field, and the necessity of a satisfactory school record in order to be accepted in the

31

school of his choice. These talks, plus the satisfaction derived from the wide acceptance by the student body of his art productions, made a rapid and positive improvement in his attitude toward school. Thereafter the same art teacher maintained a close contact with the student throughout his high school career. He became an outstanding art editor of his senior class yearbook. He conducted a profitable sign shop during his junior and senior years. He eventually went through art school and is now an advertising agency art director. The art program and an understanding art teacher saved this boy from being a failure in school, adjusted him to his environment, and certainly were enormously important factors in the establishment of a satisfying professional career. It is doubtful if any other subject could have salvaged this youngster, who was meant to be a vocational artist.

Some art educators have made rather extensive claims for the ability of art to develop and improve our conduct and, in fact, our whole democratic way of life. These claims are probably exaggerated. "The influence of art on our conduct, and through that on the political and social environment, is indirect. By making each individual a richer, more understanding person, art does influence our life of action, but the moment art tries to influence conduct directly through moral precept, it loses its true value. Such lessons are better taught through other media."[11]

Art and psychiatry

The position of the art teacher has been tenous in the defense of some of the claims made for art education—especially in the area of art and psychiatry. Stress in art education should be placed on direct benefits. Some of the published claims for art education are so thin and abstract that they weaken our whole position.

Art educators cannot hope to arrogate time or aims that rightly belong to other areas of the curriculum. Social sciences, math, music, languages, physical education, all have a place in education; they also contribute to overall educational development, and make strong claims for their programs. Art, for instance, cannot claim exclusive rights to the province of

A watercolor painting inspired by *music*. Done by a junior high school boy.

NYACK JR.-SR. HIGH SCHOOL

Early adolescents are generally interested in drawing the human figure. Drawing with a direct oil painting brush and crayon technique necessitates the elimination of unimportant details.

NYACK JR.-SR. HIGH SCHOOL

32A

Expressions inspired by music tend not to be realistic interpretations.

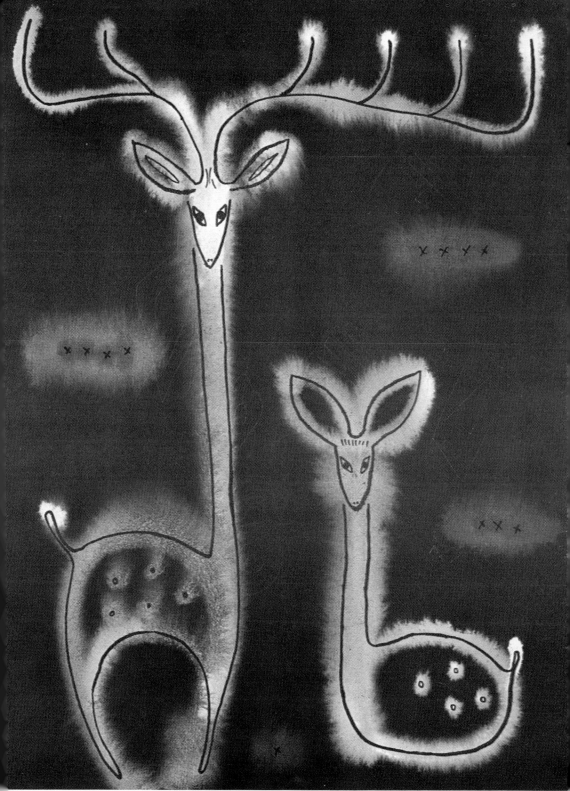

Creative imagination and an unusual use of media combined to present this delightful, naive interpretation of "Christmas Eve".

emotional release—witness a teenage jam session, or the satisfaction of expression some students derive from dressmaking, cooking, science experiments, or enthusiastic participation in sports.

The relationship between art and psychiatry, and the employment of school art as a therapy are areas, which more than any others, needs exploring today. Some art educators have stated that "the art teacher should have foremost in mind the therapeutic values of art."

Psychiatry

Logan in his history, the *Growth of Art in American Schools,* indicates that narrow emphasis such as this has "given rise to slogans, timely in nature, adapted to some small aspect of the whole value of art. Certainly 'appreciation of the beautiful' was one such slogan. Today we have another, no less narrow. For its present incarnation, art education is of primary importance in 'providing an outlet for emotional tensions.' We may hope that these rather fanatic, single-track enthusiasms can be discarded as art teachers themselves reach a more inclusive, mature understanding of the arts."[12]

An art class room attractively converted into an exhibition gallery. The movable screens were made by students using iron pipe and wall board. They can be easily arranged into a variety of groupings.

NYACK PUBLIC SCHOOLS, NYACK, N. Y.

The therapeutic values of art are really a by-product rather than an aim of art education. The therapy involved in self-expression is incidental to the total educational value. In the creative process, self-expression helps to develop self-integration. "This has important implications for art education, especially for art in the junior high school. Personal integration through experiences which are meaningful and thus yield satisfaction in accomplishment is a need present at all levels, of course, but in the junior high school years the need is more acute. The arts have a special usefulness in this area, for self-expression offers not merely a means of release but also a means of self-integration though in fact only the therapeutic applications of aesthetic expression have so far had any considerable emphasis in reports . . . . There is more to aesthetic expression, however, than therapy, more than catharsis, more than release of inner tensions. Tensions can be resolved by it, too."[13]

Perhaps a great deal of the stress on art as a therapy is because some art educators have not found the real reasons for justifying art, and, knowing that psychiatrists use art as one means of identifying psychiatric problems, they have seized upon it as a means of vindicating art and present it as one of the paramount aims.

The psychiatrist works in a very sensitive field. Only those highly trained and skilled in the subject should attempt diagnosis or prognosis of psychiatric problems. The art teacher is oriented in the field of art education. It is with this field that he should concern himself.

All teachers, of course, benefit from a knowledge of psychology—a study of the mind in its learning processes. However, their slight background is not adequate to employ in the detection of pathoformic cases or in the prescription of art as a therapy.

Apparently it is established that graphic representations are of definite value in diagnosis of and therapy for the retarded or emotionally disturbed child. His productions reveal his problems to the *trained observer*, in both what he produces and does not produce.

If a teacher notices very bizarre expressions in an art crea-

34

tion he would be wise to refer the fact to the administration or to the school psychiatrist. (Referral should be just about the extent of the teacher's participation.)

Some of the factors in drawing which we are told are pathoformic are (1) marked deviation in the sequence of figure drawing, (2) repetition or erasure of parts of the figure, (3) omission of areas, (4) compulsion to do certain types of things, (5) size of the drawing, (6) reinforcement of parts. However, even for a trained technician these factors would be meaningful only if they were repeated many times. In the average art course, we seldom, if ever, repeat a given problem. Also, as drawing plays such a small part in the contemporary art program, there is very little opportunity to observe such deviations.

Many of the symptoms which would denote deviation from the normal, if repeated over and over, can happen occasionally and have no meaning whatsoever.

If an art production does cause the art teacher to feel the necessity of making a referral to a psychiatrist, or administrator, he must be certain that the child never connects the referral with his art production! This might result in restrictions in creative work of the art class. Many students would be afraid to work freely. Efforts to encourage self-expression would be seriously impeded. The knowledge of such referrals would be spread throughout the student body. Never underestimate the power of the student "grapevine."

As art teachers we have more to do than we can adequately accomplish, in trying to achieve the modest aims of art education. Perhaps we should leave psychiatry for those who are trained for it.

Reynold A. Jensen, M.D., Professor of Psychiatry and Pediatrics in the Medical School, and Head of the Child Psychiatry Unit at the University of Minnesota, takes a very definite stand on this problem. Inasmuch as he is a trained professional specialist in this particular area we, as laymen, should give careful consideration to his knowledge.

"No parent and no educator should look to the school for therapeutic treatment of emotionally disturbed children. Treatment of the mentally ill, as of the physically ill, calls for professional medical attention. Certainly the classroom teacher has quite enough to do without taking on the additional role of therapist, even if he were competent to act in that capacity, which he is not. By trying in any degree to diagnose or treat emotional disturbance, by taking it on himself in any way to decide what is wrong with the child or what should be done about it, he is likely to complicate living for all and do much more harm than good."[14]

Art vocabulary

As our program of art education develops, the students should become conversant with the art terms which are generally used and needed in social discussions concerning art—terms such as composition, etching, Gothic, mass, impressionism, picture plane, and harmony, for example. These and many similar terms will be used and defined, with students, while discussing their productions and the works of contemporary and historic artists. There is no other place where the educational program provides for the acquisition of such a vocabulary.

References

1. Moholy-Nagy, Laszlo, *The New Vision,* Documents of Modern Art Series, G. Wittenborn Inc., New York, 1947, p. 32.

2. Whitford, William G., *A Philosophy of Art Education,* Education, LX (Nov. 1939), Palmer Co., Hingham, Mass., p. 170.

3. MacDonald, Rosabell, *Art as Education,* Henry Holt & Co., New York, 1941, p. 18.

4. Rannells, Edward, *Art Education in the Junior High School,* Bulletin of the Bureau of Schools Service, Vol. XVIII, No. 4, College of Education, Univ. of Ky., Lexington, Ky., June 1946, pp. 27 and 28.

5. Dewey, John, *Art as Experience,* Minton Balch, New York, 1934, G. Putnam's Sons, p. 62.

6. Winslow, Leon, *The Integrated School Art Program,* McGraw, Hill Book Co. Inc., New York, 1949, p. 37.

7. Teague, Walter Dorwin, *Design This Day,* Harcourt Brace & Co., New York, 1940, p. 5.

36

8. MacDonald, Rosabell, *Art as Education,* op. cit., pp. 16 and 17.

9. Davidson, Morris, *Painting for Pleasure,* Chas. T. Branford, Boston, p. 4.

10. Moholy-Nagy, Laszlo, *The New Vision,* op. cit., p. 14.

11. Simpson, Martha, *Art is for Everyone,* McGraw Hill Book Co., New York, 1951, p. 133.

12. Logan, Frederick M., *Growth of Art in American Schools,* Harper & Bros., New York, 1955, p. 3.

13. Rannells, Edward W., *Art Education in the Junior High Schools,* op. cit., p. 63.

14. Beck, Robert H., Editor, *The Three R's Plus,* Univ. of Minn. Press, Minneapolis, 1956, p. 63.

CHAPTER III   FIRST THE STUDENT

Many factors are involved in organizing an effective art education program for grades 7, 8, and 9, but none is more basic than a familiarity with the physical, emotional, and intellectual development of the teenager. Successful teaching demands an awareness of what is happening in the maturation process. The young adolescent, with his peculiar drives, fears, frustrations, interests, and prejudices, presents a very real challenge. This challenge can be met only by an understanding, benign interest in the adolescent.

Art programs adapted for teenagers

Of course, understanding the student is fundamental for all teaching. However, the adolescent in junior high school is going through rapid and profound changes. The teacher must have an extensive sympathy for the learner's problems.

It is strangely and unfortunately true that the uniqueness of the teenager's developmental stage has not been universally recognized or reckoned with in art programs by the very people who are concerned with art education. Several states offer no specially prepared course in art for the junior high years. Some city and state courses of study indicate that the program is specially adapted for the student of grades 7, 8 and 9, but no emphasis is placed on the importance of understanding how and why it should be so adapted. As a result, many art teachers have failed to recognize the need of a specific program. The success of the junior high art program is quite dependent on this point.

As mentioned earlier, in many areas the elementary art program, which is designed on an entirely different basis, is merely stretched out and continued into the junior high course. This is done with no consideration for the great change in attitudes and interests which come about in the early and pre-teenage years. Still other school systems circumvent the issue with a "watered down" senior high school art course. Most teacher training institutions prepare their graduates for either the elementary or the high school level and give no special consideration to the training of teachers for the junior high level.

Problems in planning

The art program of the junior high school cannot be planned for the "average" student as easily as when he was younger. During the elementary years it is safe to assume that all students can be classified as children. Not so in the junior high school years. Here the program treats with students whose developmental level ranges from pre-pubescent children to quite mature, adolescent young ladies and gentlemen. Probably the most nearly average factor in these grade groups is the chronological age. The puberal phase may spread out over a long period. All students do not reach adolescence at the same time; some do not even reach it during the junior high years. The teacher must be aware of the fact that some of the most physically mature will be emotionally immature and vice versa. In most cases there is no definite break with childhood; a mature attitude and deportment may be unexpectedly followed by a childish outburst. All teachers and parents of young teenagers have witnessed this. It takes real patience and understanding to make quick adjustments to their great range of unexpected reactions.

The adolescent's problems

The adolescent, though only partly conscious of what is happening, has to re-adjust to himself and his changing body, concern himself with the preparation for adult economic and social life, adjust to his age mates, develop a new relation-

39

	PHYSICALLY	MENTALLY	SOCIALLY AND EMOTIONALLY
Later Childhood 10 to 13	More rapid growth—muscles expand, bones lengthen Bodies may be ungainly and awkward because of sex changes. Voice changes in boys. Girls mature before boys, but in both sexes colorless hair appears around genitals. In girls, hips and breasts round out and menstruation may begin.	Wider range of learning and greater acquisition of skills and knowledges. Growing ability to reason and think out own problems.	May not fully accept changes in body. Grown up one minute and irresponsible and childish the next. Great desire to be part of the group and accepted by others his own age. Awakening interest in personal appearance. Growing interest in other sex.
Adolescence	Rate of growth slows down, but still rapid. Girls reach adult height at about 16. Boys grow until 17 or 19. Increase in appetite. Coordination improves. Sexual maturity is reached.	Learning becomes more specialized in preparation for job or career. Interest in abstract moral and philosophical problems, and in social questions. More critical of own learning achievements.	Moody spells, rebellion, drive toward independence. Changing relationships with parents, teachers. Interested in problems of marriage and vocation. More guidance needed, since this is time of many life decisions.

ship with his parents and other adults, accept the sex role of being a boy or girl, and contend with very mysterious sex impulses.

This is an extremely difficult period for youngsters. They need all the guidance and help that they can get from their teachers and parents. They need reassurance when they lag behind, or spurt ahead of their group in growth and in intellectual and emotional maturity. They need guidance when they seek direction, and sympathy when they make mistakes which they often feel are fatal errors. Erikson states "What the regressing and growing, rebelling and maturing youth are now primarily concerned with is who and what they are in the eyes of a wider circle of significant people as compared

Floral arrangements by students. When flowers are in season they supply an abundance of material for creative design problems.

with what they themselves have come to feel they are; and how to connect the dreams, idiosyncrasies, roles and skills cultivated earlier with the occupational and sexual prototypes of the day."[2]

Wavering of creative powers

As the maturation process unfolds, the student's attitude toward creativity seems to be affected by some change also. What, precisely, is this change? The completely free and uninhibited expressions of the young child are no longer so apparent in the young adolescent. Lowenfeld feels that "during adolescence, skills become increasingly important, and the creative approach changes from an unconscious creation to one done with a critical awareness."[3] Bannon places the appearance of a more critical attitude in creativity at an even

41

earlier age level. She states that "at about the age of nine or ten years most boys and girls become increasingly critical of their work. They want to explain ideas more accurately and with greater realism and so they feel the need of greater skill."[4]

This new interest in more skilled productions has its effect on the youngster's sureness of his ability to create, with which he was so positively endowed in his earlier years. Somewhere near the onset of puberty the emotional and intellectual development begins to become more involved in the creative process. Some art educators hold the extreme view that *creativity not only undergoes a change,* but is *actually obliterated* at adolescence. They claim that creativity in the arts ends for many years during adolescence and returns only with maturity.

Where a well planned elementary art program is coordinated with the junior high program, so that a continuity is maintained and a developmental program is stressed, children do continue their interest in creativity throughout adolescence. In cases where the children leave elementary school with a feeling of sureness about their ability to create and a healthy interest in art activities, there will not be any noticeable difference in their interest in creativity on the junior high level. If the elementary program has not kept pace with the developing child, the changes in emotional and mental attitudes accompanying the physical growth, in early teen years, will cause a wavering of the creative powers. The Pennsylvania Art Education bulletin states that the ". . . spontaneous imagination of the small child is replaced by the more controlled thinking of early adolescence. As a result of this change, many children during the adjustment period hesitate in attempting to express their creative thoughts and ideas."[5] Although they may "hesitate," they do not "lose" interest. There seems to be little doubt that the teacher, with a comprehending approach to the learner, and a program which provides for a challenging use of forms, materials, techniques, and skills, can maintain interest in artitsic creativity throughout adolescence.

Winslow notes that ". . . the sometimes apparent lack

42

of creativeness on the part of junior high school pupils is due, not to any innate lack of ability on their part, but rather to a lack of the proper psychological approach on the part of the junior high school art teacher."[6]

Schecter stresses the necessity of pleasant rapport and understanding. "Good personal relations with adolescents form the basis for eliciting creative work and provide the best chance for developing and influencing them."[7]

Good Rapport

Emotion, imagination, and aesthetic sensitivity

The choice of approach here will determine success—or failure. "In both sexes, adolescence tends to bring a heightening of all emotional activity, of imaginative power, of aesthetic sensitivity to the glamour and beauty of all existence as well as to its misery and ugliness, which may never be reached before or afterward."[8]

Gaitskell rather neatly sums up this problem in his discussion of the various stages of development. "The final stage may be reached around the 'teen' age, or probably earlier. Here the pupils seem to be ready to intellectualize a number of concepts related to design. At this level, the pupils are increasingly interested in three-dimensional representation by means of drawing. Even greater realism is sought by many, both in the proportions of related objects, and in the use made of tints and shades of colour. As adolescence approaches however, different personality traits increasingly influence expression in art. Those having tendencies toward extroversion pay close attention to the appearance of things and to a factual interpretation of events. Those who lean toward introversion tend to give greater emphasis to personal reactions, and are likely to express the emotional qualities in situations. This final stage has been called the level of 'realization,' for here, if the pupil has been properly taught, he should be in the full stride of expression. He will bring a reasonably mature personality into play and his emotions, as well as his intellect, will govern his creative output."[9]

Stages of art development

The Baltimore art bulletin presents the following study

43

of the ". . . characteristics of children at various levels of their growth and development in art." While it is obvious that this grouping must be done in a general way, it may prove valuable to the art teacher "to know about these salient characteristics . . . . even though too literal an interpretation of such standards might lead to restrictive methods of teaching."[10] The dangers involved in categorizing students in this way must be pointed out. We must consider these statements only as generalizations.

> The Twelve-Year-Old, Seventh Grader: This stage immediately precedes the change from childhood to adulthood, called adolescence. The individual is often both physically and emotionally unstable but extremely sensitive and discriminative in his art. He is fearful of the disapproval of the group to which he belongs, and is so concerned with naturalism that to him this is often the foremost objective of his art expression. There is also the child, however, whose creative activity may manifest itself in non-objective drawing, in which abstract shapes and colors are combined to form a pattern.

> The Thirteen-Year-Old, Eighth Grader: The eighth grade child is entering the period of adolescence, a time of extreme change and crisis. He has now come to realize that many of his reactions are immature, but wants to be accepted and treated as an adult. As his imagination changes from uninhibited to critical, he desires to produce a meaningful product. The significance of his product is still generally judged by him according to the degree to which he sees it as a realistic representation.

> Two differentiated types of individuals now become easily recognizable at this period, the visual and the haptic, and there is an in-between type that appears to be neither one nor the other. The visual type tries to attain realism in his work, and is concerned with correct appearances, true proportions and perspective. He approaches his subject as a spectator rather than as an actor in the situation which he depicts. The haptic type judges the excellence of his drawing according as to how it expresses his body feelings, and he concentrates on details that are most emotionally significant to him, he himself being the ever-present actor in the situations depicted. This latter type may use exaggerated proportions for emphasis, revert to base-line representation for special expression, select colors for their expressionistic rather than for their realistic values.

> The Fourteen-Year-Old, Ninth Grader: The ninth grade student

has reached the level where he is critically aware of his environment and of the means for expressing his reactions to it, be he of the visual or of the haptic type. He now has a more conscious appreciation of design than formerly and a keener recognition of the various kinds of representation; is increasingly critical of his own work and of the work of others. Having had the experience of using a large number of mediums he is increasingly conscious of the ones with which he feels most comfortable. He is also beginning to be interested in vocations and in the vocational possibilities afforded by art.

The changing body

One of the major adjustments that the adolescent has to make is to his changing body. In most cases there will be a period of spurting growth. Four or five inches of growth can take place in a relatively short period of time. The youngster will feel and appear awkward, as feet, hands, and legs seem to become all out of proportion at once.

Girls usually develop a year or two sooner than boys, which causes many awkward situations. The puberal phase for girls usually ends by fifteen, and for boys around seventeen. The earlier development of girls may cause them to become more interested in older boys. John, who has always considered Mary as a contemporary, suddenly finds her to be a woman, much more matured than he, and is embarrassed in her presence. Mary appears "motherly" to him and he shys away. Ruth, who has always enjoyed the boys in her class, and is not interested in dating older boys, suddenly finds that most boys in her age group seem like little children to her. She discovers that she has drifted away from her male classmates.

Boys become concerned about the development of their sex organs. Girls become conscious of, and, in some cases embarrassed by, their bodily development. This new concern with the body often results in increased interest in modeling and painting figures and portraits. Some of this is, of course, consciously or unconsciously due to sexual maturation. Careful guidance by the teacher is necessary during this period of interest in figure representation, in order that the student doesn't become unnecessarily discouraged with the results. This problem will be discussed in more detail later.

Adolescents begin to acquire bosom pals. Girls often

develop intense "crushes" on schoolmates, film stars, and even teacher. Mary will find that she can't make the simplest decision without consulting Ruth. They will work together, study together, walk arm in arm, and spend hours just being in each other's company. Some teachers and parents become greatly concerned about this, but it is usually a phase which soon passes.

Group influence and the teenager

It is often difficult for teachers and parents to understand the influence of the group on the adolescent. Group opinion is often more important to the teenager than the wishes or authority of the teacher or parent. "It is important that we see the child in relation to his age mates, and to the values by which he and they are governed at any given time. Actually it requires keen perception and a dash of humility to set aside some of our adult biases and habits of thought, and to understand and influence the child's perspective."[11]

The adolescent seeks to establish himself as a member of the group. The "crowd" usually determines what is to be done, regardless of adult opinion or pressure. Mary, who is completely feminine, and very selective in her clothing, wouldn't think of wearing a girl's blouse if the "crowd" is wearing men's shirts—and probably blue jeans too. Joan, who is so careful about color matching, will suddenly insist on wearing sox which don't match, to the amazement of her parents. Jack, who was sure a few weeks ago that suspenders were only for old men, now wears them whenever he doesn't wear a jacket. Bob, who hasn't combed his hair in the last thirteen years without a squabble at home, now never misses an opportunity to get to a mirror and slick down his locks with a comb that he constantly carries.

The struggle for independence

Many students are in conflict with their parents, which carries over into school even though there may be no conflict with the teacher. Adolescents strive for independence from adults, at the same time that they are striving to become independent adults themselves. The problems of dates, lipstick,

46

dances, automobiles, and summer camps all have to be worked out with parents, with resulting conflicts.

Art activities provide channels for the teenager to express his revolt against conventions being forced on him by parents and other adults. Success in the arts may help the youngster to arrive at a state of equality, *in his own line,* with adults.

"Primitive societies have feats and tasks which the adolescent performs to remove the stigma of 'child' and prove his adult status. In our complex society there are too few accepted tokens of maturity available to the adolescent. The adolescent is still in school, is dependent on parents for food and shelter, cannot marry and have a family, and yet very often he feels too mature for school and thinks himself capable of working and supporting a family. For many years after our young people are physically mature our society keeps them still children and this ambivalent status creates many emotional conflicts."[12]

Every art teacher almost always has to struggle with the problems of the gifted child. He is often not adjusted to his classmates. His special ability is far ahead of his age-mates; at the same time he may be lagging in social and physical development. He may be a very lonely person, regardless of his attitude of indifference. Ojemann advises that ". . . above all . . . help the child keep his gifted intellect in perspective. . . . Avoid making him feel that he is a person apart from ordinary beings and therefore entitled to special privileges."[13]

The art teacher's task of understanding 'the young adolescent is not a simple one. However, an insight into their problems and interests will help to make it possible to build a program of art which will be accepted by them and of benefit to them. There is no other way!

References

1. Olson, Willard C. and Lewellen, John. *How Children Grow and Develop,* Better Living Booklets, Science Research Associates, Chicago, 1953, pp. 24 and 25.
2. Erikson, Erik H., *Childhood and Society,* W. W. Norton and Co. Inc., 1950. New York, p. 266.
3. Lowenfeld, Viktor, *Creative and Mental Growth,* (Revised edition), The MacMillan Co., New York 1952, p. vii.

4. Bannon, Laura, *Mind Your Child's Art*, Farrar, Straus and Cuddahy, New York, 1952, p. 39.

5. Course of Study in Art Education, Bulletin 262, 1951, Commonwealth of Pennsylvania, Department of Public Instruction.   p. 25.

6. Winslow, Leon L., *The Integrated School Program*, op. cit., p. 153.

7. Schecter, Pearl, *Working With Adolescents*, Art Education Today 51-52, Bureau of Publications, Teachers College, Columbia Univ., New York, p. 32.

8. Munro, Thomas, *Adolescence and Art Education*, from Methods of Teaching the Fine Arts, Chapel Hill, University of North Carolina Press, 1935, p. 44.

9. Gaitskell, C. D., *Arts and Crafts in Our Schools*, Ryerson Press, Toronto, Canada, 1953, p. 17.

10. *Art Resource Materials for Junior and Senior High Schools*, City of Baltimore, Department of Education, 1953, pp. 13-14.

11. Ojemann, Ralph H., *The Child's Society—Clubs, Gangs, and Cliques*, Better Living Booklets, Science Research Associates, 1953, p. 4.

12. Mendelowitz, Daniel M., *Children Are Artists*, Stanford University Press, Stanford, Calif. 1953, p. 80.

13. Ojemann, Ralph H., *The Child's Society—Clubs, Gangs, and Cliques*, op. cit., p. 43.

CHAPTER IV

TEACHER'S ROLE

Here is that all-important "catalytic agent" in the process of art education—the teacher. The art program most liberally endowed with the best facilities, supplies, and administrative support will not bring forth superior, or even satisfactory, results without a topnotch art teacher.

"Teacher" is considered by many as a poor title to use for the person who conducts an art program. However, titles such as a "resource person" or "art consultant" also have connotations which are undesirable. What is really more important than the title is what is actually accomplished by the person who is directly charged with the responsibility of art education.

There is little or no difference between student ability in a school where a dynamic art program is in force and student ability in a school where it is not. The real difference is a competent, creative art teacher. Seeds which may lie dormant for several years and suddenly stem forth when given the proper environment and care can be likened to students who become stimulated by a creative, sympathetic art educator. Most adults today, unfortunately, never had the opportunity as students of participating in an art-studio environment fired by a competent art teacher.

Herbert Read's conclusion, after visiting many schools in England, was that "good results depended on the creation, in the school or class, of a sympathetic atmosphere, and to a certain extent I still think this true. But if by 'atmosphere' one means the amenities which money can buy, it is not true. The right atmosphere can exist in a village school, or in a dingy barracks in some industrial city. The atmosphere is the creation of the teacher, and to create an atmosphere of spontaneity, of happy childish industry, is the main and perhaps the only secret of successful teaching."[1]

The teacher and the community

In smaller towns and school systems the art teacher is expected to discharge many obligations in addition to regular teaching duties. You, as a conscientious art teacher, take on an importance that is almost awe-inspiring. You may be any one, or all, of the following: appraiser of all art objects, sign painter, scout craft adviser, stage designer (and builder), lecturer, photographer, guidance counselor, sculptor, ceramist, landscape and portrait painter, muralist, interior decorator, leader of the community art club, and teacher of art in the adult education classes. In larger communities, where there is more than one art teacher, you share these responsibilities with the other teachers and may hope to specialize in one or two areas.

Local citizens who make a hobby of some art activity, such as collecting, or color photography, acquire a considerable amount of knowledge and skill in their line. Each one will expect the art teacher to be conversant on the subject. The knowledge, skills, and experience needed to meet expectations of the school and the community cannot be acquired in the few years given to formal preparation for teaching. We must constantly read, observe, and create, and associate closely with creative artists and art educators in order to continue to develop and keep abreast of current information and trends in art education.

Qualities of the art teacher

The outstanding art teacher is rare, perhaps, just as are outstanding performers in any profession. There are, nevertheless, many areas in which all of us can develop and improve our effectiveness as teachers.

A Pennsylvania bulletin on art education gives the following list of significant statements about the art teacher.

50

"THE ART TEACHER AND . . . .

. . . his GIFT

Feels the importance, dignity, and worth of teaching

Should be endowed with a sensitive and creative imagination
Has a sympathetic understanding of emotional conflicts
Cultivates a sense of humor and laughs often with the pupils as well as sharing in their sorrows
Possesses a broad cultural background of experience which is constantly changing
Realizes that he is judged by the growth of pupil personality— not by excellence of art product, which frequently reflects dominating personality of the teacher
Believes that all art expressions are closely related
Is familiar with the vocational art activity world
Establishes prestige when he creates in one or more of the various media
Is an actively interested member of the local, state, regional, and national art education associations
Travels to experience original creative expressions in their appropriate settings

. . . the PUPIL

Realizes that all pupils are capable of enjoying certain types of emotional experience in art programs

Constantly provides for the innumerable individual differences among pupils
Appreciates, is sympathetic toward the varied interests of youth
Organizes groups that can work efficiently and harmoniously on group enterprises
Inspires, motivates in such areas of living as: salesmanship, medicine, business, science; never dictates or preaches
Stimulates pupil self-analysis and self-criticism as various stages of expression
Emphasizes the emotional and mental development of pupil rather than the preparation for a profession
Encourages pupil investigation which develops initiative and self-dependence
Develops techniques primarily on the basis of pupil personality; techniques merely serve expression
Believes in the pupil and guides him in developing self-confidence as he overcomes fear and uncertainty

. . . the PROGRAM

Creates an atmosphere of spontaneity in the classroom

51

Accepts the challenge of general education to vitalize everyday
life through art education

Inventories the art program from time to time to insure the
fullest experiences for the pupils and to avoid personal stagnation

Manages the classroom materials and equipment with an efficient measure of freedom

Works and associates with colleagues and laymen to promote
integrated programs in art education

Enriches the life of the school and the community through exhibits of pupil, amateur, professional, and folk arts

Never forgets his obligation to the community whose attitude, to
a great degree, determines the success of the art program

Should be associated with every direct or indirect aesthetic
expression in the immediate environment

Maintains a bibliography of the important professional literature."[2]

The teacher as an artist

Someone has written that "the art teacher should be an
artist who knows how to teach." There is a great deal of truth
in this statement. The teacher should know the thrill of successful completion of a work of art in some medium. This
implies, of course, a complete knowledge of the art principles,
and the materials, skills, and techniques with which the successful result is accomplished. A teacher cannot possibly understand student reactions to the creative processes unless he
himself has been an active participant in such a process.

Having been actively engaged in creativity means that
the teacher knows the relationships of design, color, form, line
and medium as they are involved in creative art. Self-expression can be fully comprehended only by those who have expressed themselves. Creative activities are essential in order
to avoid the teaching of art totally in abstractions.

The teacher must have a broad experience in the entire
field of art. He should be conversant with the materials, techniques, and design principles as they are employed in various
fields.

If we carry out the type of program which is generally
encouraged by art educators, we are called upon many times
to use our knowledge and skills in various areas of creative art.
Often it is necessary to demonstrate the use of tools, materials,
equipment, and techniques. This can be done only with considerable background experience.

52

A decision in the making. A beginning problem in design using colored papers. This introductory problem leads into three-dimensional design.

You must guard against the influence of our own personal interest and ability in a medium causing students to work almost exclusively in that medium. A teacher who is intensely interested in a medium will undoubtedly spread this enthusiasm to his classes. This enthusiasm has merit, but artificial student interest will tend to stifle natural interests in other areas.

For example, some junior high art programs have been exclusively composed of work in water colors because of the teacher's interest in water colors. This same type of restrictive program has been built around teacher interest in stage sets, masks, ceramics, jewelry, oils, or other media and subjects. Such limitation is, of course, diametrically opposed to the aims and objectives of art education. Every art teacher

53

need not be a *practicing artist,* but he should be a *practicing student* of art.

Teacher and student

Discussion has already been allocated to the problem of understanding the student in the successful junior high art program. However, it must be re-emphasized, lest art ability and methods of teaching be given undue importance.

The good art teacher makes use of all available filed information on each student. For instance, a knowledge of his social and economic background is essential in planning and carrying out the program.

A teacher asked each student to write a brief description of the most beautiful object in his or her home. One young man wrote, "The most beautiful thing in our house is my mother. She is tall and thin and dark and very clean." The teacher discovered, on talking to the boy about why he chose his mother, that "We don't have nothin' else in our room except an ol' beat up bed, a table an a couple of chairs."

Some students have a very limited travel experience, to the extent that they never leave their own neighborhood. In many homes there will be a complete absence of any discussion of art. These students, needless to say, have a distinct disadvantage.

Do not expect every student to make visits to museums and exhibits that charge admission, and to purchase materials which he cannot afford. It may be hard to realize, but an extra dollar, in some family budgets, just isn't available.

There are families that live in a single room, where the only work space is a kitchen table which is never cleared of food and dishes. Students cannot be expected to carry on *home projects* in an orderly manner in an environment of this kind. The teacher must make provision for like circumstances.

Leadership

Every school administrator can reasonably expect that in each classroom someone is actually *directing* the on-going process of education. That person, of course, is the teacher. Students also expect leadership from the teacher, and respect such leadership.

54

The old type of autocratic, teacher-dominated, regimented class has no place in the art studio, yet the group should be under control at all times. The busy hum of organized construction is very different from uncontrolled confusion. Students who are seriously working on creative constructions demand, and are entitled to, some semblance of order. Often the lack of order interferes with attempts to concentrate.

Many young teachers, and cadet teachers, find difficulty in being friendly with students without becoming too personal. Students must look on you, the teacher, as a mature, understanding adult and not as a classmate.

Each new group is ready to throw down the gauntlet to the new teacher to see who is to run the class. The school "grapevine" has usually already informed the students as to what the possibilities are. The new teacher in the system may reasonably expect to have every one of the old tricks tried, to see if any will succeed. The alert teacher with a challenging program to present, who is firm but not harsh, will have little difficulty winning over the average group. Rosabell MacDonald states: "When a teacher has a basic philosophy, practical ideas, and the courage to face situations she has real equipment for success in teaching."[3]

Planning the program

A successful art program must have a definite plan. In a book such as this, only guide posts and danger spots can be suggested. The plan must be evolved by the teacher himself to be valid and to maintain its elasticity and freshness. No one can prescribe for the teacher. Each person must plan according to his own interests and background, knowledge and experience, the available physical equipment and supplies, the philosophy of the course, and, last but by no means the least, the background and interests of the group. Step by step lesson plans, of course, are invalid. However, the teacher should know where each project leads to and what its educational value is. Planning insures that materials will be available for projects as needed. Many times a passing interest, which could be developed, will disappear when materials are not available as required.

55

The experienced art teacher will know the projects which are generally of interest to students. Some activities, in which intense interest may be developed, might not ever occur to the student unless he has been introduced to them by the teacher. Often projects are set up primarily so that students will have an experience in a particular area. This requires extensive teacher background.

Learning does not always result from success. Too often we are anxious to have students avoid failures, but a failure can often make a point more clearly than success. However, the teacher must be alert to the disinterest which develops in art if failures are repeated. Constant, alert guidance is necessary.

The teacher should create a pleasant atmosphere in a studio that is attractive, neat, and organized. Getting clay, sawdust, and paint on the floors or tables is inevitable during art activities, but cleaning up after a session is part of the learning process in developing an orderly life. Too often the variety of art activities is used as an excuse for untidiness. Aesthetics can not be taught through a disorderly, untidy environment, procedure, or activity.

Relaxation and recreation

The immense responsibility and task of facing hundreds of youngsters—often under challenging conditions—requires organized teaching and definite plans for personal recreation, at school and elsewhere. Even the last class in the day may rightfully expect to find a fresh, animated art teacher in the studio. This necessitates careful conservation of energies, and advance planning. Do not burn yourself out in one or two periods. (1) Organize your classes so that you are not always in the middle of the educational whirl. (2) Plan a variety of activities so that the work of each group is stimulating and not boring. (3) Occasionally, on the other hand, it is more effective and economical in time and energy to have several class groups engaged in similar projects. (4) Employ monitors and student leaders to advantage.

Plan to relax in the free time that is available during the day. Participate in stimulating, recreational activities outside

56

of school. Keep physically fit. "Many potentially creative teachers have been lost early in the game because they lacked *physical* the physical and nervous equipment for the weight of the task or the ability daily to replenish their energies between tasks."[4] The art teacher owes it to herself, or himself, to be as well groomed, neatly and attractively dressed, dynamic, and vital as possible.

Stimulation; materials, and techniques

The simple action of entering the art studio does not set off a burning desire to create. Stimulation for self-expression requires a dynamic teacher, a definite and vital program, a conducive environment, a pleasant atmosphere, and a recollection of previous successful art experiences. "Half of the teacher's work is to stand by and kindle the child's confidence; the other half is always to be prepared to present the right material and the right stimuli at the right time."[5] This is one of the most challenging responsibilities in the art teacher's activities. It demands constant thought, planning, and adjustment.

As has been previously pointed out, many students who have been creatively prolific in earlier grades now seem to lose their interest and fund of ideas. An imaginative and sympathetic approach throughout the elementary grades will tend to maintain creative interest through adolescence. If it has been dulled, a definite, methodical program is called for to restore confidence and encourage creativity. Superficial tricks copied from old-style manuals, T.V. "art lessons," or commercial art-supply demonstrations must be avoided. This is a critical problem for the teacher of adolescents.

The early adolescent naturally begins to feel less adequate in his ability to express himself, because he compares his products critically with others'. He demands to know why and how. He needs more than freedom—he needs direction in a developmental program—he needs teaching. We are required by the adolescent to teach techniques, to explain perspective and to help him gain facility in the proper use of tool and materials. However, the teaching of skills and techniques must be subordinated to and made the "servant" of creative

57

expression. Technical skill is pointless and boring even in a circus act, unless it is used to create a graceful and spectacular, or even comic, effect.

Although many art educators say that complete freedom should be given to the student, do they really practice this ideology? "We, too, believe he should be free to experiment, free to search, free to try his voice in his own song—but in all this freedom, he must feel the security of some one who understands and will guide him over the pitfalls. Why have a teacher, if she is afraid to bring to the student some of the benefits of past learning?"[6]

When a student becomes bogged down and discouraged in his process of creativity due to lack of knowledge of how to carry on, he needs help. Many times the adolescent can be directed into a satisfying effort by suggesting another similar but more suitable approach to the problem through some other medium, technique, or material. The teacher must be constantly alert to help guide the student into projects and media which will make success possible, according to the student's standard. "It is a misunderstanding of the adolescent's experience of art and a misuse of the media of art to put all the burden of learning upon him at this stage in his development."[7] This important concept will be treated more fully later on.

It is continually amazing to see the clever, creative, finished manner in which adolescents produce fascinating works of art in a wide range of materials, when provided with the stimulation and guidance of a resourceful, sympathetic teacher. In general, we do not really challenge our youth enough to bring forth the quality of work of which they are capable. It is worth the trip abroad to see the beautiful wood carving done by 12-14-year olds in Sweden, or the work of the youthful Italian sculptors and cameo makers. And, in another entirely different field, witness the almost professional proficiency in golf, figure skating, and other sports, developed by 12-14-year-old Americans.

Students' expectations

As the teacher expects certain results and reaction from the students, so also there are various teacher qualities which

58

students hopefully expect. The teacher who does not live up to valid expectations has a difficult role, which the students seem to enjoy making more difficult in their own peculiar fashion.

Students expect a strong, fair leader. They want stimulation, sympathy, encouragement, kindness, and understanding.

Specifically, in an art teacher they (1) look for a competent artist who is able to stimulate, encourage, and assist them in their creativity. They will (2) appreciate vocational guidance in the arts. They look to the art teacher (3) for advice in such areas as room decoration, art projects in other classes, stage productions, poster making, etc. They rightfully expect the art teacher (4) to dress in an attractive, fashionable manner. Students expect (5) advice with problems in creativity, but resent the arbitrary imposition of a teacher's ideas or techniques.

Students appreciate (6) the opportunities of planning programs, exhibitions, and the distribution and care of tools and materials. They expect (7) a clean, inspiring place to work in and (if encouraged,) will assist in leaving the studio in the same condition for others. They (8) understand free, creative expression which does not interfere with the creative rights of others.

The successful art teacher

The successful art teacher locks his classroom door each night with the satisfying knowledge that he has enriched the lives of his students by providing opportunity for them to engage in and appreciate the creative arts. He is a sensitive teacher—sensitive to the creative *expressor* as well as to the creative *expression*. He is ever mindful of the fact that he is more than an art instructor—he is an educator through art.

The following statements are a summation of worthwhile hints for successful art teaching in the junior high school.

1. *Be alert* to the adolescent, his attitudes and needs.
2. *Stimulate* the students' creativity and learning processes.
3. Step in and *teach* when necessary.
4. *Keep* personally *alive* in art as a creator.

59

5. *Be conversant* with current trends in both art and general education.
6. Have objectives at finger tips and *shoot* at them constantly.
7. *Believe* that art is worthwhile and enjoyable and your students will too!

References

1. Read, Herbert, *Education Through Art*, Pantheon Books, New York, 1945, p. 288.
2. *A Course of Study in Art Education*, Bulletin 262, 1951, Commonwealth of Pa., Dept. of Public Instruction, Harrisburg, p. 27.
3. MacDonald, Rosabell, *Art as Education*, Henry Holt & Co., New York, N. Y. 1941, p. X.
4. MacDonald, Rosabell, *Art as Education,* op. cit., p. 13.
5. MacDonald, Rosabell, *Art as Education,* op. cit., p. 23.
6. Gregg, Harold, *Art for the Schools of America*, International Textbook Co., Scranton, Pa., 1941, p. 22.
7. Rannells, Edward W., *Art Education in the Junior High School.* op. cit., p. 81.

A STUDENT engaged in the creative process is working at the highest possible level—intellectually, emotionally, and physically. All pertinent knowledge, experiences, and skills have to be selected and organized by the creator and funnelled into the activity of the creation. The emotions have to be brought into play before and during the creative process. A complete coordination of the technical skills and physical abilities of the creator is demanded. This process of the integration of the students' abilities is a valid justification for art in the pattern of secondary education. An art program in which the creative process is properly employed will convince those whose duty it is to endorse subjects for the curriculum.

Reportive and emotive art

It appears definitely established that the artistic personality of the student emerges with more definition during the junior high years. The art productions of the individual become more catagorized. Although everyone is a mixture, personalities can be classified roughly into two large groups— which I shall call the *reportive* and the *emotive*. Other labels are often used such as expressionist and impressionist, objective and subjective, visual and haptic. All have similar connotations.

The *reportive* type tends to present a factual record of his observations. The *emotive* type offers expressions of his emotional reactions to what he sees, feels, or experiences.

The reportive student is an astute observer. (1) He seeks

61

out details. He will have a surprising wealth of information about the appearance of objects in which he is especially interested—such as faces, historical costumes, architecture, airplanes, dresses, military equipment, etc. (2) In drawing he is pictorial. He draws scenes and objects in perspective and often in pencil outline. He usually selects subjects which can be observed or referred to. He will enjoy drawing from still-life, landscape, or the posed model. (3) The reportive type strives for accuracy and correct relationships, sizes, values, colors, etc. (4) He can enjoy working with rigid materials and has patience to form and finish them. (5) He depicts events or scenes as a spectator. (6) He represents color as it is seen when affected by light, shadows, atmosphere, distance, and surrounding colors.

The emotive type tends to create in terms of his emotional reaction to scenes and events. (1) His feelings and reactions are more important than his visual impressions. (2) He works from the imagination. (3) He finds little need for reference material to help define details. (4) Strong, expressive color is used which best portrays the emotional qualities of his ideas. (5) Deviation from and exaggeration of nature are indulged in.

The emotive type is more interested in loose, plastic materials which facilitate quick results. Copper wire, plasticene, and water colors are popular materials. Those requiring great technical skill and patience are avoided. Stone or wood carving is not as popular as clay modeling; pencil is not as readily used as charcoal. A medium which requires systematic techniques, such as linoleum block cutting and printing or art metalwork, is more to the liking of the reportive artist. He will enjoy pen and ink, meticulous oil or casein painting, detailed leather modeling, and similar techniques. The emotive artist will react more favorably to the free, accidental effects of water colors.

Some art educators categorize several other varieties of art expression. They include classical, intellectual, lyrical, mystical, and so on. For the sake of simplification, all of these can fit somewhere in the two large categories previously mentioned—reportive and emotive. We should, however, mention the *decorative* type, which is rather pronounced. The decorative student creates material which is a sort of combination of expressions. His interpretations are not as emotional or as realistic as are those of the two large groups. He stresses balance, especially symmetrical balance. He often expresses himself in terms of flat, two-dimensional design. Patterns of value or color are important to him. Nature gets reshaped into decorative but recognizable patterns. He employs symbols. Lines, masses, colors, textures get repeated or arranged primarily for their decorative quality. In three-dimensional creations, the basic form is more important than any emotional or representational quality.

Decorative type students combine the qualities of both the other groups. They enjoy difficult materials; they take liberties with color and form; they are interested in design structure; they may use reference material. These students enjoy experimentation with a variety of media, tools, and techniques. They are often interested in applied design, textile design, interior decoration, and similar projects.

The decorative type may lean definitely toward either extreme of the two prevalent types, causing a wide spread in the results of decorative production.

The combination of qualities

Classification of art types, at best, can be only very general. There is a great danger in it if teachers begin to think of one student as being definitely placed in a certain group and another student as being able to express only in his classified manner. Actually the majority are neither definitely reportive nor emotive. They will have qualities of both groups, with one element empasized to varying degrees, although most students and practicing artists lean toward the reportive side.

Lowenfeld found in testing for the two types, which he calls "visual" (reportive) and "haptic" (emotive), that "Most people fall between the two extreme types . . . . Only a few individuals have equal amounts of visual and haptic disposition . . . . 47% clearly visual, 23% haptic and 30% either received a score below the line where a clear identification was possible, or were unidentifiable. In other words approximately half of the individuals tested reacted visually whereas not quite a fourth reacted haptically."[1]

It is difficult to determine the extent to which each person has been influenced into favoring one style of expression by the type of art that he has seen, by newspaper and magazine pictures, and by teachers. Students tend to be conditioned by *reportive art* before they enter school. Parents' attitudes, pictures in the home, book illustrations, posters, newspapers, comics, magazines, and most television "art" lessons all stress realism. Perhaps we would find a more equal distribution of emotional and reportorial school art if children could be reared under the equal influence of both.

The reportive tendency seems more prevalent in older groups, where more time has been available for conditioning. In some adult art classes it has been found that the entire group created pictorially—due probably to conditioning.

It should be pointed out here that the emotive student though dominated by his emotions, is also, to varying degrees, influenced by his visual experiences and intellect. He does not create entirely from his imagination. Nor does he work without a conscious application of technical ability. Of course, also, the emotions of the reportive student, to varying degrees, are involved in the creative process of even the most factual type of production.

The importance of our being conscious of the various artistic personalities in students is that we realize that some are not as reactive to certain stimuli as others. Also, a given stimulus will cause different reactions in different students.

In the older, traditional school art program the reportive type of art was encouraged. Considerable use was made of models and reference material. Pictorial illustrations of objects and landscapes were developed. Procedures and techniques were stressed. The student whose artistic personality did not conform, usually felt disturbed by his apparent lack of art ability. He withdrew from participation; he often became a behavior problem and usually developed an apathetic, if not an antipathetic, art attitude.

The more recent school of art instruction has encouraged a more emotional type of creation. Students have been

64

A delicate, imaginative drawing done by an eighth grade girl. Color was first flooded onto a wet paper with no attempt at a definite result. When dry, a few accent lines were added to define the forms which were suggested by the accidental patterns of color.

64B

Vigorous tempera expression inspired by music.

A strong, expressive use of watercolor in a free design.

64F

Gummed squares of colored paper were used for this appealing Madonna.

encouraged to work large and freely. Deviation from real-ism has been honored. It is evident that in a creative art program there is room for many types of productions. The creative problem will have as many solutions as there are students in the class. We are not trying to develop a standard type. We are no more interested in encouraging all emotive personalities than we are all reportive personalities.

Some students thoroughly enjoy working meticulously and/or diminuatively and can make beautiful creations while employing highly developed techniques, whereas others are more likely stifled by a methodical procedure and a restriction of size and technique. The teacher must recognize the variations of artistic personalities in order to be able to interest all segments of his groups in creative expression.

In our present educational system, where uniformity is too often the goal, success in the creative arts tends to help the student to see the value of his own personal individuality. The creative art program is one of the few areas in the curriculum which *encourages and fosters the uniqueness of the personality* and its attitudes and expressions! The student gains security and comfort from his ability to express himself uniquely in some art form which conveys a meaning to others. General self-confidence is also gained from being able to engage actively in the solving of creative problems in a personal way. This sense of security and self-confidence growing out of art participation is such a valuable contribution that the general educator in the junior high school *cannot afford to avoid supporting* an extensive, creative art program.

If the student expression is a personal interpretation and not directed by outside influences it can appear realistic, mechanical, or even photographic and still be creative. On the other hand, the abstractive, *original appearing* production is not a creative expression of the student if he has been influenced and/or directed by the teacher. If it is not creative it is not art.

It is disturbing to see how many students seem to produce in a particular style of art when a teacher's interests or desires in that style are marked. Many times we see whole classes concerned with mobiles or abstract oils or some other art ac-

65

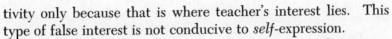

tivity only because that is where teacher's interest lies. This type of false interest is not conducive to *self*-expression.

There probably has been as much teacher influence recently in encouraging an exclusively emotive type of art as there was encouragement of reportive productions in the traditional schools of the past. Both are ill-advised.

Arousing interest in creativity

The very young elementary grade student is usually flowing with creative ideas. This interest in creativity may lose its keenness as the child matures, due to many influences. At the junior high level he needs constant stimulation which the art program and art teacher must provide.

Suggestions for simple projects

The recapturing of interest calls for a definite plan. Introduction of *new materials* and projects will be helpful. A *medium* which is easily controlled and which produces startling results may be used. *Color* is fascinating to most people. By all means avoid a project which will not have general appeal. In the majority of schools visited during an entire fall term it was found that drawing and/or lettering, taught on a very narrow basis, was used as a disciplinary measure to get classes "in line." Developing a creative art program on this basis is impossible.

A suggestion for a successful introductory problem is to make folded color blots on paper and then develop them into simple abstract designs. This project, obvious as it is, does not require a long span of interest for its simplest completion and works out well with all students. The imagination is stirred. Rather exciting results are insured. All get off to a stimulating start merely by the accidental results of folding the paper on the color blob. Further development can be engaged in by spattering on additional color spots or by wetting part of the paper to encourage mingling of the colors. At the completion of a problem of this type it is possible to tack up for exhibition each one of the results on an equal basis. For some students this may be the first time that they have seen their work favorably shown in relation to the work of the

66

more talented members of the class. It becomes obvious to each that it is possible to be creative, to enjoy it and to meet with reasonable success.

Some other ideas for simple and rather exciting projects are:

1. Potato block printing.
2. Simple mobiles using abstract shapes of colored paper.
3. Ink sketching on moistened paper.
4. String painting.

In doing these projects, supplies and tools must be arranged for in advance so that there is no delay in beginning. Projects can be easily completed in one period of forty to fifty minutes. The experience of seeing unexpected results so easily produced will stimulate further interest in art activities. More complicated creations, which require more skill and longer attention span, can be introduced gradually as interest develops and the abilities and art personalities of the students become known to the instructor.

The blot design problem might be followed by developing a similar design or an entirely new abstract, realistic, or decorative form. After this design has been painted boldly in rather thick tempera and is thoroughly dried, a coat of india ink can be painted over the entire paper. Then the whole sheet, which is now black, can be washed off under the faucet and the original design will reappear with a most pleasant and unusual new surface treatment. This problem may be done in full color or in white paint only on white paper. The latter is probably more fascinating for the student. First his design is all white; then the ink coating leaves the paper all black; then the running water, as if by magic, will produce a black and white design.

A few problems of this type will excite the imagination of most, if not all, students. Now the teacher must be alert to the various interests and abilities which manifest themselves. A wide choice of projects and materials must be available. The efforts of the various art personalities must be recognized and encouraged. The teacher should help students avoid the pitfalls of certain techniques, materials, and problems which will prove discouraging. The teacher must always be ready to

67

guide when necessary, *encourage* when advisable and *teach* when required. In these early stages, all problems which demand a long attention span, or any systematic series of processes and difficult techniques, should be avoided.

Each failure at this point tends to re-affirm a student's belief that he cannot be successful in the art program, and it will be practically impossible to stimulate subsequent active participation by this student. However, the course must not be so simplified that it is devoid of challenge and development. For then all students will begin to doubt and misunderstand the value of art.

At adolescence, the more reportive-minded students begin to lose interest in products of the imagination. If they are to create, visual stimulation is necessary, such as working from nature, architecture, models, and still life. The handling and use of tools and materials in three-dimensional projects is extremely valuable in maintaining creative interest. Boys show greater interest than girls in mechanics, science, and spatial relations. So they are usually more interested in and better able to handle tools and rigid designing materials. Most boys will be receptive to creative art if the program provides for their interests in this area. The availability of challenging materials in the art program is one answer to behavior problems which plague so many junior high art teachers.

As there is a wide spread in development of junior high students, the more immature students will not yet be so interested in the technical problems of creativity. Nor will they be so interested in nor able to work with tools and difficult techniques.

It has been previously pointed out that most students have a combination of qualities of both the reportive and emotive types. There is a problem in trying to keep the student from becoming excessively engrossed in one or the other extreme type, to the detriment of his work. All students should be encouraged to enrich their own expressions. For example, when, in drawing, too much stress is being placed on transcribing nature, a student could be encouraged to engage in linoleum block printing, which does not adapt itself so readily to realistic expression. Ceramics or wood carving can be valuable aids in encouraging a student to compose freely. Reportive art must be a personal interpretation rather than a mere transcription if it is to be creative.

In drawing or painting, when a student fails in attempts to give form to objects and needs perspective, then the teacher can help him. If, however, a student enjoys working on two-dimensional projects and has little or no interest, or ability, in perspective, he can be encouraged by seeing some of the works of artists who produce successfully without concern for perspective—such as Paul Klee or even Grandma Moses.

Creating with materials will enable some students to realize that lack of drawing ability need not be a deterrent to spontaneous self-expression.

The teacher's background in creativity, materials, and processes will help students across difficult spots, and avoid disappointments or discouragement. For instance, a student with some knowledge of the pliability of aluminum might choose this as a medium to be used in a project which requires shaping and soldering. As it is almost impossible to solder aluminum, the teacher could suggest copper, which also shapes easily and can be readily soldered. Or the student might be encouraged to try soldering both aluminum and copper before choosing material for the problem.

"Avoiding discouragement" also means that the student should be free to experiment in the use of materials or techniques.

Art experiences during early adolescence

As has already been pointed out, it is important to promote the special interests and attitudes of the young teenager. The type of social relations possible in the art classroom studio is high for this age level, because boys and girls learn to work together, and to respect each other for their accomplishments at a time when team sports tend to separate them. The opportunities for self-expression, in a choice of media, help many youngsters to "work out" their antagonisms toward adults and society in general. It is healthy to get annoying emotions out of the mind and onto the finger tips in the creative process.

At this level, boys and girls will enjoy designing emblems

and insignia for their clubs, church groups, classes, and home rooms. The alert art teacher will capitalize on those new interests which are peculiar to the teenager. For instance, the development of young bodies will cause considerable interest in making sculptures, drawings, or paintings of the figure, and portraits. Some students have an unusual facility for figure work and can carry it on to a quite mature level. However, figure work is extremely difficult for most students and they can easily become discouraged in this area. This is especially true if the student is attempting a realistic approach. Depicting the figure well enough to satisfy most teenage artists is often impossible. Care must be taken that not too much stress is placed on this area.

As boys and girls develop there comes a new found interest in the opposite sex. Romances bud, flower, and fall almost daily. Boys and girls will spend hours of loving application to the job of producing a gift for a "friend." (Often the length of production outlasts the period of the romance.) The art teacher can profitably harness this newly stimulated interest in craft production.

Are all of us artists?

Frequency of art ability appears in individuals in the same proportion as that of other highly specialized abilities. In other words, there are no more students who are finally to become successful artists than there are those who are to become outstanding track stars, renowned medical specialists, or ace war pilots. Vocational success in the art field requires an unusual amount of natural skill, iniative, ability to concentrate and organize, ideas and concepts, and a driving urge to create. Being any kind of artist requires much more than a creative flair.

Many books have been produced with titles and themes which suggest that all of us are artists. All of us are not artists. The word artist, in any field, means something extraordinary, and must not lose its meaning.

As art educators of young adolescents we must be constantly aware that we are not trying to create a mass of artists and that only occasionally do we find a student who has the inherent qualities and abilities to become an artist. It is terribly unfair to any youngster to promote the idea that all can be artists. The day of reckoning finally comes for him. Moholy-Nagy stated that everyone is able to participate in the arts and to "give form to his reactions in any material (which is not, however, synonymous with 'art' which is the highest level of expression in any period.)"[2]

The significance of the creative expression

Being engaged in the creative experience of self-expression calls for a concentrated involvement of one's intellect, emotions, and technical skill; it demands far more than emotional release and exhibitionism. Creating requires industry as well as excitement, intellect as well as emotion, knowledge as well as experimentation, discipline as well as freedom, resolution as well as release, method as well as flair, consideration as well as impulse. Only when we have a blending of all of these qualities do we have a valuable, educative, aesthetic experience resulting from self-expression. Only then may we call it creative expression. Too often art educators have placed too much stress on areas such as emotion, flair, and release, and ignored the other qualities involved in creativity. It has been this unbalanced emphasis which has caused many school executives to become prejudiced against art and has made the task of the creative teacher more difficult and in some cases practically impossible. Often, without understanding modern art, a sort of pseudomodernism has been carried on in the art classes. As a result, many clichés, tinged merely with the characteristics of contemporary artists, have been introduced.

Many so-called art programs would not be possible if Alexander Calder had not designed abstract patterns which carousel in space—and this is no reflection on Calder's work. Of course, the works of Calder, Picasso, Mondrian, Cezanne, Matisse, and other pioneers has been of inestimable value to progress in art. By their departure from the influence of the traditional past, and their experiments in form, color, design, and drawing, artists have broken loose from many restrictions. However, this freedom has resulted in an epidemic of meaningless form and color. "Form does not reside in aimless blobs of paint nor in reckless brushwork . . . . after all, form cannot be brought into being without tangibility, integrity and dimension."[3] In other words, mere departure from the traditional does not insure a work of art—modern or otherwise.

This misinterpretation of modern art, and the lack of training and discipline in creating, has caused concern among many artists, critics, and educators. Ralph Pearson writes: "Free emotional expression without the discipline of design is unbalanced confusion."[4] Some painters have wandered so far from the real meaning of creativity that it caused Thomas Craven to jeer at the expressionists slogan, "True feeling makes true art." This "has become the painter's panacea and his silencing answer to inquiring laymen. This notion lends authority to that brand of self-satisfaction which parades as genius; it allows for every imaginable kind of stupidity, and lack of knowledge; and raises the scratches of freaks and incompetents into the ranks of the masters."[5]

The struggle in the creative process

The free creative expression of every young child is of value to him because it is a challenge to him—whether or not he is to become an artist. Art continues to be of general educational value only as it continues to challenge the best of the individual's emotional and mental processes.

All children on the elementary level can make a serious and meaningful approach to art, even though the activity may appear to some adults as a play activity. Children are serious about it and completely captivated by it. The simple application of color to paper or squeezing clay into forms is a challenging and absorbing activity for youngsters. As the student matures, his creative expressions need to embody more than experiments with materials and meaningless emotional presentations. The developing adolescent needs to be challenged at his own level.

The more mature and meaningful art creation requires something beyond the impulsive expression of the child. First, the production must be visualized. Then the processes of analyzing, selecting, and producing take place. There must

72

A study in value relationships with wet watercolor technique. This problem can be done effectively with black paint or with color.

be a balance between the emotional impulses of the idea and the rational, logical method of effecting the idea. The process of expressing the original concept through materials into an external form is a difficult and often a painful one. It is at this point that many students are tempted to deviate from the original concept and accept a result which does not require a continuation of concentration and struggle within the limitations of the medium. This factor is probably the difference between the average student and the artist. Dewey stated, "What most of us lack to be artists is not the inceptive emotion, nor yet the merely technical skill in execution. It is capacity to work a vague idea and emotion over in terms of some definite medium."

Dewey further stated: "Struggle and conflict may be themselves enjoyed, although they are painful, when they are experienced as a means of developing an experience .... There is ... an element of undergoing, of suffering in the large sense, in every experience .... It involves reconstruction which may be painful. Whether the necessary undergoing phase is by itself pleasurable or painful is a matter of particular conditions. It is indifferent to the total aesthetic quality, save that there are few intense aesthetic experiences that are wholly glee-

73

ful. They are certainly not to be characterized as amusing, and as they bear down upon us they involve a suffering that is none the less consistent with, indeed a part of, the complete perception that is enjoyed."[6]

Henri Matisse also stressed the importance of the quality of being able to meet the challenge of the struggle in the creating stage. "In art, the genuine creator is not just a gifted being, but a man who has succeeded in arranging, for their appointed end, a complex of activities, of which the work of art is the outcome."[7]

It is during the creative process that the art teacher has an important function. It is a difficult and delicate task to keep alive the student's interest and still draw out of him the very best that is in him, so that he will be able to appreciate most fully the success which can be had only by overcoming the problem-solving hardships involved in the creative processes. The young student may need counseling in organizing his conception, selecting his medium, and employing his technique. He needs encouragement so that he does not give up the struggle before he arrives at his predetermined outcome. The teacher does not, however, personally come in contact with the creation, nor does he direct the course of the construction. Gaitskell points out that: "Provided with inspiration and materials the young learner, like the artist, must be left alone to come to grips with his problem. The teacher in stepping aside at this point is performing a further necessary function."[8]

"When an individual is able to see the process to fruition, he has a tremendous return in the form of a renewed faith in his own original vision."[9]

 Creative art does not mean free self-expression any more than democracy means unbridled freedom. "Sheer self-expression requires no artistic form."[10] The creator must conform to the restrictions of his own concepts, his tools, his medium, and to his own level of emotional, intellectual, and aesthetic development.

Successfully working out a creative expression is one of the most satisfying activities in which a student can participate. The rewarding sense of accomplishment will encourage continued participation in creative art.

Waterproof ink on wet paper was used to draw this design. If additions are desired when a design of this type is dry, the paper may be moistened again without disturbing the original drawing. Colors may also be added.

Drawing as a creative process

Drawing can and should be a creative experience. Unfortunately, drawing has become an unacceptable stepchild in art education. In the past the traditional art program consisted primarily of drawing. Drawing then meant as nearly an exact copy of nature as possible. Nature was set up as the standard art criterion. If it looked natural, it was art. This, of course, allowed nothing for the imagination. Because of the way in which drawing was interpreted, it was almost eliminated from the program of the art teacher with the advent of the modern art concept.

Yet drawing is a perfectly natural means of expression. Most anyone, finding himself unoccupied, with a pen or pencil

75

available, will doodle a decorative design or a rendering of some object. We know that very young children—even before being exposed to parental "art education"—will scratch drawings into dirt with a stick, or will make linear expressions on a sidewalk or wall with chalk or a stone. Thousands of years ago—before the coining of the phrases *art education, modern art,* or *self-expression*—primitive man drew representations of people and animals on the walls of his cave. Buck, in explaining his "House-Tree-Person Technique" of psychoanalysis, states that drawing was chosen as the medium of expression because, "It is a relatively primitive one."[11] It has been a mistake to overlook this perfectly natural means of self-expression in the art programs. Probably the strongest argument on the side of drawing in the art program is simply that *most students like to draw*.

Modern art education, while carrying the banner of self-expression, has placed such rewarding emphasis on abstract or non-realistic art that the student who naturally would have found an expressive outlet through drawing has been embarrassed into a poor, artificial attempt at "freeing" himself in directions which have been away from drawing.

Although drawing is one important element in art education, we, of course, must not stop there, and we have no important reason to start there. Unfortunately, we still find hundreds of art programs which consist almost entirely of drawing. In fact, many art teachers still entitle their art program "drawing."

If drawing consists merely of imitation, it becomes a handcraft rather than art. "Any transcription of surface appearances, however skillful, is a mechanical process, hardly a creative one. . . . not the transcription of experience but the translation of it into the language of form is the function of the creative process."[12]

Young adolescents have a real interest in drawing. If drawing is carried on as a means of interpretation it is a creative experience; it can be developed into a valuable and important part of the creative art program. It can be exciting, challenging, and educational to the emotive as well as to the reportive type of student.

76

The height to which the technical skills of adolescents can be developed is shown in these superior examples of metal work and a ceramic animal.

Drawing should certainly not be confined to the pencil, which is probably among the least exciting of all media. Drawing can be done with pen on wet paper, Chinese brushes, stiff oil brushes, stylus on scratch board, light-colored chalks on black paper, crayons of all kinds, charcoal, in such materials as leathery dry clay or dry plaster, and in countless interesting manners. Drawing can also be combined with various other techniques and media.

Many students will appreciate the drawing experiences which will enable them to express themselves adequately in an illustrative manner. Opportunities to apply this ability present themselves in almost every other subject area of the curriculum. Drawing ability also gives the student a method of making visual records of things which he has seen.

The seeing process involved in studying an object enough to make a drawing of it helps to intensify and cement the experience of having seen it.

Drawing is an important factor in the process of learning some of the things which develop an appreciation of the works of artists and designers. A student who has drawn an interpretation of an actual architectural detail, for instance, has a much better appreciation and understanding of its character, struc-

77

ture, form, and texture than does a student who has looked at it without thus *seeing* it.

Certainly drawing should not be overlooked as an important creative and educational element of the art program.

Technique—the vehicle of creative expression

The technique is the method by which a person puts his material into the form that expresses his mental concept.

Too often we hear that techniques are taught as the need arises. This is logical. But we must be alert to the need when it becomes evident! It is not fair to let a student struggle with a problem to the point of discouragement when the knowledge which the teacher could impart would help the student to pass over the hurdle and facilitate progress with the creation. This does not imply a teacher imposition on the student's personal expression.

A student came to her art teacher and said she knew what she wanted to do but needed some advice in using a new medium which she felt would best express her idea. Lack of teacher guidance here might easily stifle experimentation in other new materials, and might seriously affect further interest in creativity.

Techniques are not very difficult to teach or to learn. However, as Walter Dorwin Teague states, use of a technique doesn't guarantee results: "The results depend on the skill of the men who use it."[13]

The technical skills necessary for producing an oil painting are rather simple, and an adolescent can easily acquire all the craft necessary. Anyone who can mix paint and paint a chair can learn to manipulate pigment to make a painting. All over America hundreds of thousands of paintings are produced annually which are technically satisfactory as far as craftsmanship goes, though very few works of art are created.

If a student's manipulative skills fall too far behind the development of his critical ability he feels incapable and becomes discouraged. Techniques help him to bridge this gap. We must constantly work to keep alive the inborn urge to create.

Often the striving for perfection causes the desire for

78

ASHLAND PUBLIC SCHOOLS, ASHLAND, OHIO

Wood carvings in walnut. They have been painted with a mixture of beeswax, turpentine, and linseed oil, and then rubbed down with a lint-free cloth. Both of these pieces were gold key award winners in the regional contest in Cleveland and were judged in the National Scholastic Art Awards.

instruction in techniques. Care must be taken that students do not become so involved in technical processes that they are merely super-imposed on the creation. This can result in techniques hindering self-expression rather than facilitating it.

In the creative art program the teacher has the pleasant opportunity of stimulating the imagination and the intellect, counseling in the organization of the idea and the selection of materials, teaching the skills, techniques, and principles neces-

79

sary for production, providing encouragement during the creative struggle, and enjoying with the student his thrill of successful accomplishment in the most satisfying area of education—that of the creative process.

References

1. Lowenfeld, Viktor, *Creative and Mental Growth,* (Revised edition) New York, The MacMillan Co., 1952, p. 232.
2. Moholy-Nagy, László, *The New Vision,* op. cit., p. 17.
3. Pitz, Henry C., *Martin Johnson, Seeker of Forms,* American Artist Magazine, Watson-Guptill Publication, New York, March, 1954, p. 24.
4. Pearson, Ralph, *The New Art Education,* Harper & Bros., New York, 1941, p. 11.
5. Craven, Thomas, *Men of Art,* Simon & Schuster, New York, 1931, p. 501.
6. Dewey, John, *Art as an Experience,* Minton, Balch & Co. (G. Putnam's Sons), New York, 1934, p. 41.
7. Matisse, Henri, article, *The Nature of Creative Activity,* Education & Art, UNESCO, Paris, 1954, p. 21.
8. Gaitskell, C. D., *Art Education During Adolescence,* Ryerson Press, Canada, 1954, p. 25.
9. MacDonald, Rosabell, *Art as Education,* Henry Holt & Co., New York, 1941, p. 36.
10. Langer, Susanne, *Philosophy in a New Key,* Harvard Univ. Press, Cambridge, 1942, 1951, p. 216.
11. Buck, John N., "The H-T-P-Technique," *Journal of Clinical Psychology*, Brandon, Vt., October, 1948, p. 3.
12. Rannells, Edward W., *Art Education in the Junior High School,* Bulletin of the Bureau of School Service, Vol. XVIII, No. 4, College of Education, Univ. of Kentucky, Lexington, June 1946.
13. Teague, Walter Dorwin, *Design This Day,* Harcourt, Brace and Co., New York, N. Y., 1940, p. 2.

THE ART program is a very positive and definite affair. It has specific aims and objectives. There are areas to be explored, imaginations to be stirred, things to be created, skills and techniques to be developed, knowledges to be acquired, and appreciations to be gained. The art teacher must have a well-organized plan in order to make most prudent use of available time so that all possible benefits are assured.

There are certain elements which appear over and over again in all art productions—color, form, line, mass, texture, space, value, etc. These should be explored, analyzed, studied, and employed. The awareness of these design elements will tend to free the student from any tendencies toward imitative coyping and will provide some definite factors for use in creative work.

Moholy-Nagy pointed out in his description of the Bauhaus school how essential it is to have a plan and sequence of training to develop artistic talent. "Therefore it is indispensable, in human development, to pass through all the stages of elementary experience in every field of sensory activity. Little by little man attains his own way of expression, and finds his forms."[1]

All art productions must be the student's own to be of value. This does not mean that all students must work on different problems at the same time. But all must be able to express in their own way their own experiences. With some of the large classes that are assigned, it would be chaotic for a teacher to attempt to have all students work on different

81

types of projects at the same time. This is not expedient or practical. There is just not enough time for the teacher to approach each student daily to check the value of each project and assist when guidance is needed.

The teacher will need considerable more background information in all areas than can be presented in a book of this type. Reference books on specialized subjects should be familiar to teachers and available to students.

The suggestions on color projects are presented here more extensively than is most other material in an attempt to illustrate how this and similar problems could be developed.

No specific program of study can be planned for a teacher. Each must work out the course material and sequence of problems with his own pupils.

Developing the course outline

Here is a proved method of developing an outline of a series of units with the pupils:

(1) On the chalkboard, make a list of the art areas in which the students indicate interest. (2) Through discussion, point up the various information, skill, and design elements incorporated. Then (3) a comprehensive outline for a semester's or year's activities can be developed on the board. Students will appreciate this opportunity to organize their own course. They will know what areas they are to explore and will anticipate with pleasure projects which have personal appeal.

Of course, the teacher has the responsibility of being sure that adequate emphasis is placed on units which will be of most benefit to the over-all plan and of suggesting units which might be overlooked by the students due to lack of background experiences.

A considerable amount of creative thinking will be involed in the discussions developing the course outline. It may carry over several days. If most students have had an interesting, creative art experience in preceding grades, this planning can profitably be done during the first days of the course. If they have had an unfortunate art background in preceding grades, it is wiser to begin the course with some simple and exciting problems in order to invole the students in a satisfying creative experience.

The teacher will have to be ever conscious of the objectives of art education and the over-all plan so that the class does not become bogged down in problems for an undue period of time, which will limit the available time necessary for other projects basic to the success of the program. This often takes diplomatic maneuvering. However, it is easily possible for a class to miss a great many essential art experiences if too much time is used on any given part of the program.

The following units of work are ones which have repeatedly come up when outlines have been worked out with students on the junior high level. The imaginative use of these units has resulted in hundreds of students completing a junior high art course with a basic knowledge of art, a highly developed appreciation, and with their creative abilities stimulated and uninhibited. Of course, no one of these units can be developed in complete isolation from all the others. There will be considerable overlapping. Also, there is no way of knowing in advance which unit most logically is to follow the introductory problem. For that matter, there is no way of determining which is the most logical place to start! It is probably safe to assume that perspective drawing and/or lettering (where many art courses start—and where some also end) is probably the most unexciting place of all. Color will certainly have been suggested by the students as an area to explore and usually is a satisfactory point of departure. So we might begin with color.

Color

Color may be introduced in an unlimited number of ways. One method might be to stimulate discussion by some of the following questions:
1. What is the brightest color in the room?
2. What color suggests quietness?
3. What does "feeling blue" mean?
4. How many colors are there in the room?
5. Does the color red suggest a warning, and why?
6. What color do you like best?

Follow up by suggesting that each student do a mingling with water color or tempera on wet paper. Students may also do a brayer print, a finger painting, or a string painting. These finished experiments should be tacked up on the wall for inspection. It will be noted that the ones which have the strongest patterns of design will be those which have *value contrast*. Here we learn about one of the three important properties of color.

Value

Value is the lightness or darkness of a color. Demonstrate how value can be controlled by adding white or black to the color so that a range from full value to white and/or to black can be created with any given color. Now suggest the making of a value chart, running from the lightest tint to the darkest value of one color.

There is little originality in this problem, but many students will be surprised and pleased to learn that they are able to create any value of any color. (Incidentally, they will also learn how to lay smooth washes of color.)

Decide upon the number of steps that are to be included in the controlled color scale. Twelve to eighteen is a satisfactory number. As a very definite and even step gradation is desired, it is advisable to make about double the required final number of steps, and discard the ones not required after the final grading of value is done.

This problem can be completed best by having each student design a very simple shape, cut it out and trace around it 25 or 30 times on a piece of paper. These shapes can then be colored with the various values. The tracing should be done with a heavy line. Paint the value over the pattern area without stopping within the lines. The dark lines will show through the dry paint, if the paint is not applied too thickly. This leaves a flat, smooth color value within each shape.

Start with a small amount of white tempera and begin adding very small amounts of color—painting a sample of each value as it is mixed—until full strength is reached. Then begin to add black to the color for the darker values. If the student begins with the full strength color and attempts to reduce its

84

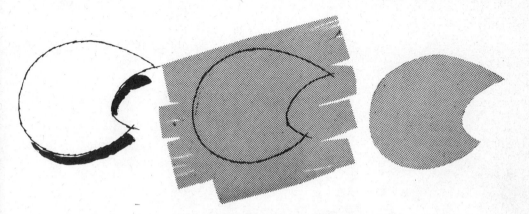

value by adding white to it, he may end up with a quart of mixture before the lightest value is reached.

The shapes can now be cut out on the lines and the ones which show a steady gradation of value from black to white can be selected. These can then be arranged in an interesting way on a sheet and neatly mounted with rubber cement.

Follow this with a discussion of how values are used in various fields, such as interior decoration, costume design, textile patterns, linoleum, automobile color schemes, magazine illustrations, and painting. Have the students collect examples of these.

Now the students should develop an original design, in any desired manner or technique, working with this newly found ability to create strong patterns of value in a monochromatic scheme.

The teacher should cover the care of brushes, paint, paint jars, and other equipment as this unit develops.

It will be noted that a problem of this sort includes discussion, exploration, experimentation, creation, and appreciation. Hence it is a valuable educational experience in art.

Hue

A problem of the type suggested above will stimulate interest in knowing more about color control and development. Creating various hues from the primary colors will prove fascinating. It might be introduced by having students see how many hues of any one color gradation, such as green-blue

85

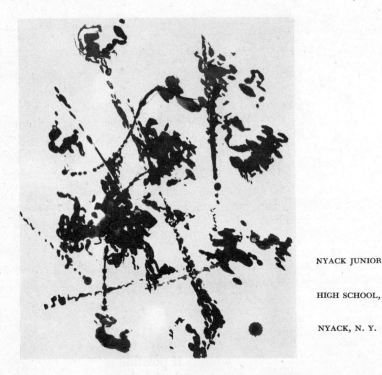

An experiment in creating with abstract patterns in black and white by an eighth grade girl. Disassociation from nature forms frees the student for personal interpretation in space designing.

to violet, they can find in old magazines. Clip small samples of these and mount them on a sheet. When they are observed it will become evident that, in addition to light and dark values, colors are varied by the addition of other colors. Some students will know about the primary hues and how these combine to make all other hues. A simple, quick demonstration will show how the whole gamut from yellow through oranges to red can be created. Have students experiment with the primary combinations.

Though there has been criticism of the use of the color wheel in art teaching, a more effective method has not been developed. It does serve the purpose. It is economical of time and readily understood.

Color wheel

86

It is not suggested that making a color wheel is a creative problem. It is a learning situation which results in an accumulation of knowledge about color that provides the student with an added tool for use in his creative efforts.

In making a color wheel, students will find that getting each sample of color painted, cut out, selected, arranged, and mounted can be most expediently done by using the method described for the value chart.

When these color charts are tacked up, we are ready for a considerable amount of discussion about color. Bring out the differences between warm and cool colors, and how they are employed by industry as well as artists. Dangerous areas, moving parts of machines, fire alarm boxes, and other items are painted warm colors to make them conspicuous. (Note the color of school buses.) Cool colors reduce eye strain, make contrasts possible, and give the feeling of quiet and repose.

Mixtures of colored pigments, and of colored lights, produce different results. For example, a mixture of red and green pigment produces a neutral gray, whereas green and red light produces a yellow white. If possible set up a demonstration of this. An interesting method is by the use of slide projectors. Make 2 x 2 slides of colored gelatins. Use two projectors to project overlapping colors on the screen. (A demonstration of after-images can also be done effectively with a slide projector.)

Have students experiment with color relationships by placing discs of colors upon a variety of different colored backgrounds to see how colors seem to change due to the relationship to other colors.

Most people react similarly to color so advertising artists base their selection of colors upon this tendency.

Discuss the ways color is or could be used more effectively within the school building. The class will be able to gain and share a considerable amount of information as to how color is best used in clothing, housing, and industry. A discussion of make-up and its intelligent use by adolescents is a natural development.

Now creative problems should be introduced to put to

87

use some of this information. Suggestions are: abstract design using full color, seasonal painting featuring warm or cool colors, posters, interior color schemes.

Always keep in mind the significance of art appreciation. The teacher must be ever mindful that the development of artists is not the objective, but we can justifiably aim at developing an appreciation and active use of art in all students. As they participate in art problems and begin to understand the challenges and contributions of art, we must be alert to point out the relationship of their activities with the productions of artists in the past and present.

Intensity

The same color clippings previously used may be used in this unit, or we might pick out all the red colors in the room. Decide which one is the brightest. It will be noted that some colors appear to be the same hue but have greater or lesser intensity than other colors. It may be obvious to some students what has been done to each color to cause this. Experimentation and discussion will bring out that opposite colors on the color wheel tend to lessen the intensity of each other when they are mixed. This is a most important fact which most students will have occasion to use many times in their lives—especially as "do-it-yourself" interior decorators.

Suggest that students make an intensity chart by using any two opposite (complementary) colors. To either of the colors add a very small amount of the complement and continue to do this until the paint becomes a neutral gray. Now start with the other color and add the complement until this also becomes a neutral gray. These steps, which have been painted at each stage of the mixing, can now be cut out and so arranged that there is a continuous progression from a color at its full intensity to its lowest intensity, through neutral gray and on into the fullest intensity of the complementary color.

Making such charts may seem ritualistic, but students need it and enjoy it. They become engrossed in seeing the colors change, and gain a unique satisfaction with their demonstrated ability in color control. There seems to be no other effective means of achieving the end. The experiments will result in

88

amazing advancement in the use of refined colors, which opens up an almost unlimited range of color for student use. Undirected exploration might be carried on for years without achieving color information which can be solidly learned in a few class periods of organized study.

The amount of time to be spent on problems which will include application of new color knowledge will have to be determined by the teacher and the class. Be sure that everyone has ample opportunity to make application of his newly gained knowledge to his creative expressions, so that he will be stimulated and extended while his knowledge of color broadens.

DESIGN

Line

One of the simplest and most challenging design elements to begin with is line. A suggestion is to have students draw and discuss the various types of lines that they can think of. Have them draw lines which suggest speed, stability, anger, uncertainty, calmness, a dancing movement.

How can we make an interesting design if we are limited to black, vertical, oblique, or horizontal parallel lines? How can we provide variety? (By grouping, spacing, width of lines, texture of lines, etc.) Have students make some line designs, using only parallel lines. A cut-out blank the shape

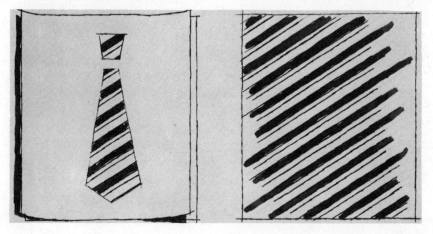

of a tied necktie, a pair of shorts or a peasant skirt could be placed over some of the results to see what sort of textile designs they would make. This same problem may be worked out with full color, single color, complementary colors, or values of one color or black.

Another experiment is to make a decorative design in a given area by using only one continuous line of varying widths. Or create a border design, using lines to emphasize rhythm.

Mass

Using the geometric or free form, solid-colored shapes make an abstract design. As these designs are observed, it will be noted that variety is needed to provide vigor and to avoid monotony, and that similarity in shapes and colors is needed to avoid chaos, or to develop integration.

Problems may be introduced which will illustrate both formal and informal balance, dominance, and rhythm.

The teacher should constantly point up the relationship between the design elements and principles used by the students, and those in commercial posters, paintings, magazine illustrations, architecture, interior designs, and historical design.

Texture

Suggest that students experiment to discover the interesting ways that paint can be applied to paper without using the brush in the conventional manner so that they may discover the use of the brush for dry brush, spatter, and stipple. Sponges, textiles, screens, corrugated board, and many other devices can be used to transfer color to the paper. Color can be applied through stencil shapes and around templates. Color thus applied can be more provocative for the beginner than that which is applied in the usual manner.

A conventional style of painting already done may be re-created in several textures. Or an entirely new design can be developed especially for texture experiments.

Here again the job may be done in limited color or in full color. Be sure that the students are developing a refined sense of color and design as they progress in their problems.

90

Colors come out of the tubes and jars in their raw state and *Blended* in almost every instance need to be blended to make pleasing combinations. Raw color is generally used only in very small quanities. Doris Lee employs a very refined color palette in her fine paintings. So does Al Parker, a popular commercial illustrator.

Next, actual materials could be used for the textures in designs. This problem provides for unlimited creativity and originality. Most unusual materials can be combined to make *Collage* completely satisfying results. Care must be taken here that materials are *organized* into designs and are not mere collections of cast off material, or junk. The materials should be composed with a sense of style, using all of the student's knowledge and abilities gained from previous problems.

Here may be a very logical point at which to begin working with materials in three dimensional design. See the following chapter.

DRAWING

Drawing is a perfectly natural means of expression. Most students will be interested in drawing and in learning more about it. This unit should teach him how to represent three-dimensional form on a flat surface. This representing of space, distance, and form can be intensely interesting. For some students it is the most exciting area of art. Recall that Ucello was so animated with his discovery of the principles of dilineating form in three dimensions that he stayed up all night working at it.

Drawing does not have to be taught with a list of rules and restrictions, as a species of geometry. Nicolaides in his *Good method. James To See!* excellent book on drawing states: "The job of the art teacher, as I see it, is to teach students, not how to draw, but how to learn to draw. They must acquire some real method of finding out facts for themselves lest they be limited for the rest of their lives to facts the instructor relates."[2]

In addition to teaching us how to represent structurally, drawing helps to train the eye to see. Rannells places great emphasis on this. "What art has to say is addressed to the eye. What the eye sees depends on what the eye is trained

91

to see . . . . The training of visual skills is the first responsibility of art education. All other goals depend on it . . . . Drawing is also a means of graphing ideas, of putting down the image of what has been imagined, or materializing thought in visual terms; it is useful, also, to be able to 'read' these 'signs' and know or sense their meanings."[3]

Henri Matisse also stressed visual skills. He stated: "Thus, for the artist, creation begins with vision. To see is itself a creative operation, requiring effort. Everything we see in our daily life is more or less distorted by acquired habits, and this is perhaps more evident in an age like ours when the cinema, posters and magazines present us every day with a flood of ready-made images which are to the eye what prejudices are to the mind."[4]

Through discussion and learning how to *see*, many of the mysteries of linear perspective will be erased for the students. Hold a large disc, or the top of a round wastebasket, horizontally on eye level and students will see that a circle in this position appears to be as a straight line. By moving it above eye level, and below it, they will observe that the line becomes an ellipse and that it becomes a wider ellipse as it moves farther from eye level. Many will never have observed this before.

They can now practice to advantage, drawing curvilinear objects above and below eye level. Use vases, jars, jugs, pails, bottles, and pitchers.

An interesting demonstration is to place, in advance, on the end wall of a long corridor a large red disc of paper where the ceiling and floor lines all appear to converge when seen from a given position in the hall. Then take the students into the hall and have them observe how the lines of the ceiling appear to go down and together and how the floor lines appear to go up and together. When standing at the previously determined spot they will be interested to see how all lines appear to extend to the red disc.

Have the students recall how, when they stood at the edge of the shore of the ocean or a large lake, the water seemed to rise from their feet and meet the sky at eye level. The sky seemed to come down to meet the water. Perhaps the horizon can be viewed for this effect from the classroom window.

92

Have students observe a cube. How many sides can be seen at one time? Some students will at first declare that they can see four sides. Move it into various positions. They will all finally agree that at most, only three sides can be seen at any one time. Also note that in some positions only one or two sides can be seen at once.

In perspective drawing objects are depicted as they appear and not as they really are. Objects appear much smaller as they go back into space. It is often almost impossible to believe how different objects can appear. Have students hold up their thumbs at arm's length and compare them to the heads of classmates a few seats away. Many will for the first time discover that their thumb appears as big as the other student's head. Show them how to measure with the thumb and a pencil at arm's length. Have them measure floor boards or tiles at their feet from a seated position and then compare this measurement with similar objects at the other end of the room. They will find that the distant ones seem to have been greatly reduced.

Exercises of this type will emphasize how important it is really to *see* when drawing and not to draw unthinkingly.

Students will enjoy drawing various parts of the school interior, and landscapes outside the building.

Some may seem to have a real desire to learn to draw in perspective, but cannot quite acquire the ability necessary to transpose the solid form onto a two-dimensional surface. Usually these students can be helped by having them observe an object or landscape through a piece of glass and then trace the image with a crayon onto the flat surface of the glass as they see it. This can be done on the window or on separate piece of window glass which has the edges protected with a strip of adhesive tape. Usually one drawing in this manner will enable almost anyone to understand how three-dimensional objects have to be interpreted on a flat surface.

Drawing of objects can be made more interesting by using large brushes, Chinese brushes, charcoal, colored crayons, or colored chalks on black paper. Use large sheets of newspaper (even printed paper can be effectively used) and do many quick drawings of objects after studying the forms

Student

gesture

drawing.

NYACK JR.-SR. HIGH SCHOOL

enough to become familiar with them. Make memory drawings of objects. Another interesting project is to have students come to the chalkboard and draw objects which they cannot see, but which are placed in their hands behind their back. The whole class will want to try this. Merely by touch, even small details can be determined and delineated.

Suggest a problem using a motif to work out an abstract, interpretive line rendering for an all-over pattern. Any motif, such as flowers, heads, cubes, fruit, etc., may be used.

Mechanical Drawing

While the cube was being discussed, it was very likely that the area of working drawings and the development of surfaces came into the conversation. At some time it should be further discussed and studied. This unit is concerned with how to depict the surfaces of objects so that they can be dimensioned. Shapes are drawn as they actually are. Discuss plan and elevation drawings. Demonstrate the use of the T square, compass, and triangle. Make simple working drawings with the aid of instruments.

94

This phase of drawing will be of value to every student who ever wants to put down on paper an idea of a room plan, house plan, piece of furniture, or any solid object. All of us at some time need to do this. Working with instruments will be especially valuable to those who plan to do anything in the field of interior decoration, advertising, architecture, mechanical drawing, or designing.

If the school has an industrial arts shop or a mechanical drawing department, make a class visit there to see how finished drawings are made and how they are used when objects are made from them. Make use of visual materials such as blueprints, house plans, and machine drawings.

Figure Drawing

All junior high classes will want to spend some time on figure drawing. However, the stage of critical development of most junior high students is such that they are not readily satisfied with their own results in figure work. Some become unduly discouraged. This is especially true if the approach is a very realistic, photographic one.

There are many ways to begin figure work. Each youth can decide on a particular action that he would like to portray. Then each can stand up and go through the movements of this action, to begin to "feel it." Then, with broad strokes of a flat crayon, depict it. Or the whole class might decide on a particular action and each person render his own interpretation of that same action. A model (student) could pose in an action pose for a few seconds and then all make a memory drawing of it.

Try *gesture drawing*. Have a student pose briefly in some extreme action pose. The others try to record their interpretations of the pose through a series of very sketchily drawn lines or brush strokes. Only the direction and action of the body and extremities, in a masslike form, are sought out in this type of drawing. Small details are unessential.

Contour drawing. In this approach the student seeks out the lines which best express the form of the figure. This can be done with a pen or a soft pencil, which will give a smooth flowing line. Do directly with no erasures.

95

Posing as a model provides an opportunity for some to acquaint themselves with the duties of the profession. Those who are thinking of becoming professional models can be brought in from outside the art class to pose for experience. Often we find young persons with outstanding abilities in this line. Girls will enjoy posing in party dresses or sport clothes. Boys will gladly pose in athletic costumes or historical costumes from the dramatic department.

Another interesting approach to figure drawing is to have students look continuously at the model while drawing the contour lines on the paper. Only a few minutes should be provided for each drawing, in the styles mentioned above. Make some volume drawings by using a continuous line to form a compact series of ellipses creating the volume of the head, and continue this type of structuring on down the body, doing the torso and extremities the same way. Avoid details— and disappointment!

For those who are interested, longer poses may be used, and drawings developed more completely. Try a variety of media.

Portraits

A portrait unit will be popular with many, but realistic likenesses are difficult to draw, even among trained artists. Care must be exercised by the teacher to avoid disappointments. Only those who have a natural flair for figures and portraits will be able to accomplish their aims.

Making silhouette "portraits" often proves interesting as an introductory activity in this area, because of their simplicity.

Figures in illustrations

The above problems can be followed by rendering figures in composed groups to show some particular action such as a football game, a square dance, a pep rally, a campfire group, or a beach party. Girls will want to do some fashion figures and boys will enjoy doing athletes, servicemen, and historical and fictional adventure characters.

Figure drawing will undoubtedly stimulate interest in doing figures or animals in clay, wood, wire or paper sculpture.

96

A very sensitive rendering of a posed figure. It was completed in color and then covered with india ink, which was later washed off leaving a most interesting textural quality.

96A

Strong but controlled color is used in this simplified interpretation of a suburban dwelling.

A free color mingling done in tempera on wet paper. The picture was later developed along the lines suggested by the original mingling. This type of problem tends to loosen up students who become too involved in details.

96F

A crayon etching by a twelve-year-old boy. The base color is covered with a second color which is then removed in some areas by scraping.

A still life group expressed with sponge and tempera by a Nyack junior high school girl.

96H

*Pen and ink, and watercolor washes combine to give form
to this sensitive interpretation.*

If drawing is taught as here suggested, the outcome should
be an individually creative interpretation of objects, figures,
and landscapes. If tightness develops, it may be of value to
try some minglings. Have each youth study these minglings

to decide what the color patterns suggest to him. Then he may add details in color and/or lines to complete the rendering of the figure, object, or scene. This usually helps to "loosen" his work while drawing.

As has been previously emphasized, the sequence of problems cannot be determined in advance. It may be that figure drawing will switch the interest of some to posters for a dance or a football game. Then exploratory work can be done in the area of advertising and poster art.

Perhaps puppets or marionettes will be an outgrowth, and then stage sets, designed in their connection. It is also likely that interest will turn to painting as a result of the problems in structural representation and figure drawing. The making of linoleum block prints of heads, still life, or landscapes may lead into the development of a unit in the graphic arts.

In any event, proceed from the student's current interest to develop problems or units based upon the original course outline. The principles of design and color which have been previously covered will make for more beautiful and creative productions as the course progresses. In all units make use of as much visual aid material as possible to kindle interest, inspire greater efforts, and open a broad view of art phases. Use slides, films, magazines, and prints. Visit studios. Invite artists to lecture, demonstrate, and exhibit. Visit exhibitions. Integrate art projects with other areas of the curriculum and school activities. Make art live.

Presentation and techniques

As the course progresses and student-artists gain in knowledge of design principles, they will be better able to make interesting presentations. Their creations should be placed, mounted, or matted in an attractive manner. Their names should be carefully lettered and located on two-dimensional work. Neat cards can identify other work. Neatness should be insisted upon.

Encourage committees to arrange interesting displays of work as it is completed. Setting up exhibits should serve as creative design problems in themselves. Do not display so much work at one time that the exhibition space is cluttered.

98

Each class will be interested in seeing what is being produced by other groups, and each will benefit by the opportunity.

When the knowledge of a particular technique will free a student to carry on with his own creative expression, the technique should be taught. However, do not allow techniques to dominate the type of work that is created. Encourage experimentation in various media and techniques.

Be sure that students are developing good work habits. The studio should be cleaned up by each class after it is used. The leftover litter from one class is not conducive to creativity of another. Aesthetics cannot be effectively developed in messy surroundings.

CLEAN-UP

Painting

Most students will be eager to do some painting. Some will be quite serious about it.

This unit may evolve directly from the preceding units. It may grow from an exhibition of painting or a field trip to a museum, or a movie about an artist or a painting. It can be introduced by painting a picture to express an emotion, or based on such events as a circus or a football rally. Make full use of the extensive visual aid material in this field. Visit museums, galleries, and studios where possible. Survey the broad field of painting. Study and discuss examples of the important schools of painting. Review the elements of design and color as they apply to some of the paintings available. Study at least one artist and know about his life, times, contemporaries, education, and style of painting.

Boys will be especially attracted to Leonardo Da Vinci who, in addition to his great paintings, produced many interesting inventions. He was probably the first to experiment with airplanes. His rope-making machine and marble saw have not yet been improved upon. He made designs for breech-loading cannons and air-conditioning units.

Grandma Moses appeals to girls. She spent about seventy-five years of her life as a homemaker before she began painting and is now about as well known as any painter. The adaptation of her paintings for fabric designs has made her even more popular.

President Eisenhower's interest in painting attracted many to this field. General Grant, and President Jefferson Davis of the Confederacy, did satisfactory painting, as did William Tecumseh Sherman, whose paintings hang at West Point in the United States Military Academy. Peter Hurd, noted painter of the southwest, was also once a West Point cadet. Whistler is another artist whose formal studies began at West Point. The drawings made by Winslow Homer as a war artist during the civil war are often a means of introducing fine art painting to junior high students. Getting to know about the life of any one artist will serve as a little island of departure for those who may later wish to learn more about various artists.

Have students make some experiments in various schools of painting and see if the class can identify the schools. Perhaps a few lessons in portrait painting will be desired. Explore as many media as is feasible.

Casein is a medium which can be used to advantage in schools whose periods for painting are very short. Casein mixed with water on peel-off palettes makes the clean-up time almost negligible. It can be applied to almost any kind of paper, illustration board, or beaver board. So it is economical. Water color is also an inexpensive medium and easy to clean up. However, it is not a good study medium and very few people can fully exploit it and use it successfully. Tempera is much more easily handled on this level.

Mural painting provides opportunities for social development. Boys and girls can work together as equals, at a time when interest in team sports is inclined to separate them. The less skilled person also plays a valuable part in a large production. Large scale work provides a satisfactory sense of achievement which is different from that which results from the smaller works of individuals.

Theatre arts

Any one of the preceding units may lead directly into the study of theatre arts. Or begin with a discussion of the use of dramatics in the cultural expression of the past and present. Television has enabled many youngsters who do not live in metropolitan areas to see the dance and drama.

100

Junior high school puppeteers intensely preparing for the "On stage" call.

101

"The Loon's Necklace" might be an effective movie used as an introduction to this unit. This can be followed by the making of papier-mâché masks.

As has been said, constructing puppets or marionettes and theatres for them is usually of interest. Committees can work effectively on this unit. There are jobs which will appeal to the interests of almost everyone: script writing, stage designing and building, set designing, making the heads of characters, creating costumes, building furniture and props, making the figures and controls, and lighting effects.

The story or event being studied in the English or history course may serve as the theme for a show.

If possible arrange for each class to work on a full-size stage set. Each individual will derive a great sense of satisfaction from contributing in some way to a big stage production.

In almost every locality someone can be located who has considerable experience in theatre make-up. Arrange a demonstration of how this is done and note the exaggerations of color that are necessary because of strong lighting effects on the stage. If possible witness professional stage lighting.

Small models of stage sets can be built by groups. These can be constructed in cardboard cartons. Each group can do one set for each act of a selected play, or for complete plays selected by each group. This is an absorbing activity.

Girls will be especially interested in designing costumes for stage characters.

As the program of art develops, we find how important it is to note carefully how much time is being spent on each unit. We must remain aware that our program is to provide opportunities for exploration in many areas and that we are trying to develop an appreciation for the broad field of art. We should not concentrate on any one phase of art expression to the exclusion of others of importance.

Commercial art

All of us have more contact with commercial art than with any other type. We constantly see and use products created by the industrial designer. Incessantly we observe

102

Junior high boys engrossed in building a model stage set.

advertising in magazines, newspapers, television, car cards, highway billboards, posters, store windows, and display cases. Much of this is very good advertising art. Some, of course, is rather poor.

Advertising art

The mission of the advertising artist is much different from that of the fine artist. Although he works with the same tools, techniques, media, and design principles, he is bound by rigid controls. He has to meet deadlines. Regularly and consistently, he has to create work which will have general appeal. His art has to reproduce well with sometimes very cheap reproduction processes.

103

If possible, plan a visit to an advertising agency or to a commercial art studio. Try to procure copies of an advertising campaign in all stages of development. Discuss in class the number of people who are involved in making a magazine advertisement, including the art director, copywriter, sketch artist, typographer, printer, letterer, illustrator, photographer, and engraver. Note how each part of the finished job is done by a specialist. Most young persons do not realize that a whole team is necessary to produce a magazine advertisement.

Have students make a rough layout for a full-page, full-color ad for some particular magazine. Look at several magazines and newspapers to analyze the layout style of each.

Lettering

Although a large percentage of the copy in advertising is type set, usually the captions have been hand lettered. In posters nearly all of the lettering is by hand. Lettering takes a considerable amount of practice. One has to be so familiar with the alphabet styles and the tools used that he does not hesitate in forming the letter. It requires a definite swing. Good lettering cannot be done by working slowly and laboriously. Study effective advertising to see the simple and direct lettering which is generally used. The beginner has a tendency to try fancy, difficult-to-read, and often "original" styles. This is not conducive to legible and effective lettering, which in itself, is not meant to be a creative part of advertising art.

Work out some simple words in a plain, sans-serif alphabet. Require good spacing and crisp, neat execution. Use the best brushes available. Demonstrate how lettering can be worked out on tracing paper and then transferred to the final sheet for inking in. Do not use stencil letter kits!

A measuring gauge made with a piece of paper will prove helpful to keep strokes of letters uniform. This is simply done by using a very fine pencil point to mark off on the edge of a small piece of paper the width of stroke decided upon for the letters. The gauge is then moved to check the width of all strokes of all letters. After the lettering is roughed in and spaced freehand, the T square and triangle may be used to check vertical and horizontal lines.

104

Students should now apply this knowledge to a simple problem, such as making a folio cover with their name, direction signs for the corridor, or other one- or two-word jobs.

Folio Cover. Good.

Posters

Many art departments find it difficult to avoid becoming a poster factory. Poster making is an important unit in the art program but there are many other essential experiences in art education. The Pennsylvania Course of Study expresses a realistic viewpoint regarding requests for posters: "The response to these requests should be organized from the point of view of number and time so that they provide for the optimum creative and mental growth of the pupil. This over-all direction and control will avoid the exploitation of pupils by individuals or groups dominated by other than educational purposes."[5]

Discuss the elements of a good poster. Show samples of the work of outstanding poster artists. The aims of a good poster are to *attract attention* and then to be *easily and quickly read* in order to sell an idea or product. Posters are usually placed where people walk or drive past. Therefore the shorter the message the more surely it will be read. A motorist watching traffic while driving past a highway poster at 50 mph cannot read more than he can see at a glance. A pedestrian usually is preoccupied with other thought.

Most orders for school posters request too much lettering. A poster is different from a magazine advertisement, which is usually read by a person with a few minutes to spare. Poster advertising, to be effective, must be brief.

A poster attracts attention by its color, its design, and/or by its illustrative material. A picture is not necessary but usually helps attract attention.

In almost every community it is possible to visit a business place which does outdoor advertising, truck lettering, and posters. Many helpful hints will be picked up here. The production of legible, fast lettering may be observed. Note the use of both round and chisel point brushes. See how both single-stroke and built-up lettering is executed.

Design and paint a poster for a school dance, a game, or

105

some club or church affair. First make small idea sketches and tack them up to see if the design is powerful and attractive. Select the best one and, if no alterations are necessary, proceed with the final poster.

Story illustration

The story illustrator works with a different purpose and with different limitations from those of the fine artist. The illustrator must portray the characters and present an interpretation of the mood of the story. He is almost always restricted in medium, technique, color scheme, size, shape, and type of reproduction.

Study illustrations from books, newspapers, and magazines. Note that some illustrations are vignetted, some are divided by center page margins, some are in halftone, some in line, and some have half the illustration in full color and the part on the other page in one color.

Those with figure-drawing ambitions can choose characters from a story and do an illustration. Decide in advance on the medium, technique, size, and colors to be used. Perhaps an illustration can be made for use in a school paper or class book. If possible let some students do wood cuts and linoleum cuts for reproduction by a printing press.

Other commercial and fine art

If time permits, discuss the areas of costume design, fashion illustration, textile design, package design, interior design, window display, and cartooning. Have each student select one of these areas for a project. The display and discussion of completed problems will help all to gain in concept and appreciation of commercial art work.

Another highly successful plan for providing an opportunity to gain an acquaintance with other fields of art—both fine and commercial—is to have reports by committees. Have the class divide up into small groups and each one select some phase of art to study and present to the class. Demonstrations and illustrative material should be included in the presentation. Guidance may be necessary in the selection of the topics and especially in the preparation of the outlines of the reports.

106

This unit can be successfully accomplished only if there is ample reference material in the art room, and school or community library. It is always fascinating to discover the areas in which the students have developed hobbies or interests and in many cases amazing amounts of information. Out of this unit have come interesting and almost professional presentations of paper embossing, wood engraving, effects of colored lights, graphic arts, mosaics, basketry, use of natural dyes in weaving and many other exciting phases of art.

An interesting testing program can be carried along with this unit. Before the presentations begin each committee can hand in five questions related to its subject. At the close of the unit a true-false quiz can be given including all of the questions. This will serve to help establish how much information has been imparted. The committees will all be anxious to find out how much information they have gotten across in their own particular unit as indicated by the scores on their unit.

HOME DECORATION AND DESIGN

Here is a phase of art education which has a direct application for all of us. Whether a student lives, or will live, in an apartment, a rented house, or a family home, his living will be enriched and engraced by the application of art principles.

The introduction of the paint roller, water soluble printing inks, and silk screen processes makes it possible for almost anyone to design and print his on fabrics for upholstering and draperies, and to redecorate his room, home, or apartment.

Many adolescents are interested in changing their own room from the province of the less appreciative child to that of the maturing person.

"How would you redecorate your own room if you had complete freedom of operation?" This question will usually bring forth statements of problems in interior decoration. Some will have windows that are awkwardly placed, ceilings that slope, or are too high or too low, or rooms which are too dark or small. The girls want a feminine atmosphere; the boys something sporty.

Discuss how the principles of design and color can be ap-

107

plied to help correct many of these deficiencies without structural changes, which are seldom possible.

Use of mirrors will help small rooms seem larger and narrow rooms seem wider. A long narrow room can be made to appear more nearly square by painting the far or short walls a warm, advancing color and the near or long walls, a cool, receding color. Reduction in apparent height can be effected by painting the ceiling a warm color and bringing the color down on the side walls for a foot or two. Windows which are too squatty can be given height by adding valances with the bottom of the valance beginning near the top of the window. Tall windows can be made to appear lower with a box valance painted the wall color, to cover the top portion of the window. If the wall is papered, the valance can also be papered. Pipes, radiators, and electrical outlets can be made less conspicuous by camouflage—making them the same color as the background. A large unbroken wall can be made more interesting by the use of a large patterned wallpaper or by hanging groups of pictures. Large pieces of furniture can be made less conspicuous by blending their colors with the wall colors. Dark rooms should have draperies which hang at the sides, clear of the window opening so that no daylight is shut out. The right choice of paint, wallpaper, and fabrics also helps brighten a room.

Interior color schemes

A simple way to work out a pleasing color scheme for a room is to start with a well-designed piece of fabric for a chair cover or drapery. This will contain a harmonious combination of colors worked out by a skilled designer. Decide whether the walls are to be cool, as generally used for a southern exposure, or warm, for a northern exposure. Then the proper wall color can be selected from the fabric. It may need to be made lighter or darker. Individual wall colors may be desired. Different solid colors for chair cover fabrics can also be selected from the original fabric. In a large room, a striped material containing several colors of the color scheme can be used on at least one chair. Accent notes of strong color may be introduced in lampshades, vases, pillows, etc.

108

Discuss floor plans and furniture arrangements. Conduct experiments with the hanging of single framed pictures and arranging groups of pictures.

Students can collect an abundance of·reference material on interior decoration from companies which sell tiles, carpeting, flooring, furniture, paint, wallpaper, or architectural plans. Home decoration magazines will prove ready sources of reference material.

Have class members make an elevation drawing of two walls of their own room, or a room in the house which they would like to redecorate. Make a list of essential and non-essential furniture and equipment which is in the room. Then proceed with the working out of the color scheme and rendering the room in full color. Some students may wish to use a corrugated box with which to make a model of the room with model furniture. A few parents, when they find that a sound plan for decoration has been worked out, will help make a reality of it.

Excellent use!

Other problems connected with home decoration which might be worked out: (1) Make a lamp base in wood, plastic, metal, or ceramics. (2) Design and make a valance, book shelf, book ends, ash trays, waste basket, lamp shade, magazine rack, mobile, or stabile. (3) Design and print material for draperies, pillows, or upholstery. (4) Design and weave place mats, rugs, or table runners.

Discuss the exterior design and decoration of the home and its relationship to its natural environment and other buildings.

In suburban areas, the planning of the yard and garden may be profitably explored.

Graphic arts

Making multiple prints is always interesting. The outcome is a greater ability to appreciate commercial processes and the works of the graphic artist. Students also learn to make reproductions of their own work for decoration, illustrations for school newspapers or yearbooks, greeting cards, bookplates, place cards, or programs.

This unit can be introduced with a simple printing proc-

109

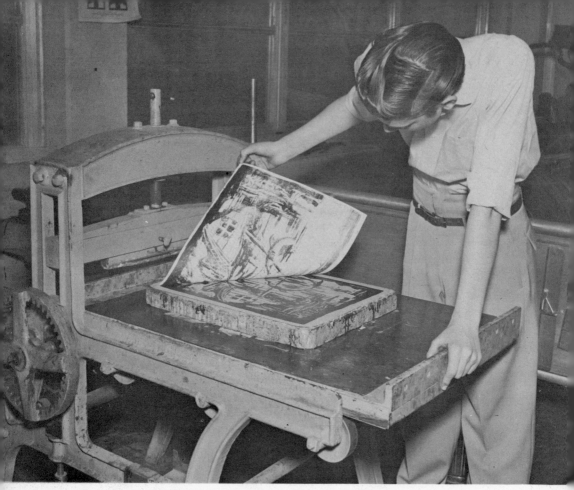

A student inspecting a lithograph on stone.

ess that can be done in any class studio. Use water solvent inks which are easier to clean up. Printing can be done with a sliced potato or carrot, or an art gum eraser. Suggest a very simple design such as an initial, a decorative abstract pattern, or a floral shape.

Interesting designs can be made by using cut shapes of cardboard. The patterns may be torn to give irregular edge effects. A thin layer may be removed from the cardboard for other textured effects. Several colors can be used in one design.

Fascinating designs can be printed directly from a rubber brayer. Patterns of color are created on a sheet of aluminum or glass. The brayer is then rolled over this pattern in one

110

complete roll. The ink can then be transferred directly to the paper. If simple chalk designs are made on the paper first, the ink will not adhere and so a line design will appear running through the rolled design. Unlimited effects are possible in brayer printing.

Brayer

Linoleum printing is done rather simply and easily. Have students experiment with small pieces to get the feel of the medium and to discover various ways of cutting. Following this a demonstration may be done to show other ways of cutting. Be sure to demonstrate holding the block at the near side and cutting away from you so that there is no danger of a slipping tool injuring a hand. A bench hook will help to hold the block while cutting.

Linoleum

Nearly everyone will enjoy making Christmas cards. If lettering is used, keep it very simple, as it is hard to cut. Be *sure* all lettering is reversed on the cut. This advice comes from sad experience.

If the budget does not permit the purchase of linoleum, scraps can usually be procured from local shops. Perhaps a student has a father who has some connections with such a firm. Umbrella spokes can be sharpened and used as cutting tools as a last resort. Foot pressure serves as an adequate press. An old clothes ringer also prints well.

Scraps of softwood can be used for block printing.

Show samples of other methods of printing, such as lithog-

This jovial design was made by an eighth grade girl with burlap, string, and cardboard. The print was done by rolling the original design with printers ink and offsetting it onto a piece of newsprint.
LA CUMBRE JUNIOR HIGH SCHOOL, SANTA BARBARA, CALIF.

raphy, etching, serigraphy, and monoprinting. If materials are available, try some of these processes. Visit galleries, studios, and printshops. See how type is set and plates are made from line drawings and photographs. Boys will be fascinated by typesetting machines. If possible, visit a photo-engraving shop to see how colors are separated and how color plates are made. *Encyclopoedia Britannica* offers an excellent film on the story of printing.

Silk screen prints are easily made with minimum equipment. Organdy can be used for the screen and the printing frame can be simple. Japanese tapestry weave silk works best, and its durability makes it the most practical and inexpensive screen material in the long run.

Church art

The churches are an excellent and too often neglected, source of visual aid material. In small communities, church art helps to make up for a lack of original art works available. In larger communities, the variety of church artwork calls for special attention. Many times a church will provide the only examples in the community of excellent pieces of wood carving, wrought iron, silver and gold ware, statuary, mosaics, tapestry, stained glass, paintings, stone carving, and historical and modern architectural details.

The exquisite colonial architecture of some of the old New England churches is a joy to behold. The Spanish mission churches directly affected the style of architecture of our southeast and southwest coastal towns. In many areas the churches of all denominations represent outstanding examples of contemporary architectural interpretation.

The connection between American history and American churches is a most fascinating area to explore. The signal which started the movement of American troops in the Revolutionary war was hung from the tower of a church—Old North in Boston. Many churches were used during the American Revolution and the Civil war as hospitals, objectives, and in some cases the physical substance representing the culture of the enemy on which the opposing force felt it should spend its wrath.

112

Architecture

Homes and public buildings are a part of our everyday life. They have been built in response to human needs. Many influences are involved in the examples of architecture which we see about us. In the past most of our architecture was influenced by historical designs. Our contemporary architecture is more definitely influenced by function, construction materials, and modern tastes. Some communities have readily accepted and encouraged modern design. In others, the influence of traditional taste has resisted the development of contemporary architecture.

Some of our historic buildings, though hundreds of years old, retain their beauty. Fine design endures in popularity. Some of our modern architecture will live on. That which has been unduly influenced by cost, materials or exhibitionism rather than by sound design principles will soon perish, as did much of the architecture of the past.

Historical architecture

The Parthenon, probably the most famous building in the world, has been called the one perfect building. At any rate, it has been highly influential, and was built to last. This building was completed more than 400 years before Christ. It is a great tribute to the designers and builders that, although severely damaged in battles, much of it still stands today, after more than 2,000 years.

Discuss this building with the class. Show slides or photos of it. Have students try to find buildings in the community which have been influenced by the Parthenon design. Many of our public buildings and homes show this relationship.

Study the various types of columns which were used by the Greeks. Find examples of these in the community. Perhaps adaptations of them will be found in the school. Several students will discover that their own front porch or entryway has columns. See how many columns can be counted on the way to school. They will be found in both urban and rural areas. In West Virginia and Kentucky some of the log cabins still in use today have white columns holding up the roofs of tiny porches, in attempts at majestic dignity.

113

Discuss and show other details of architecture which were used by the Greeks. Show the similarity and differences of Roman architecture. Study pictures of the Pantheon. See how Thomas Jefferson's Monticello was influenced by Roman architecture. Have students find examples in the community and photos of buildings with domes, bridges with arches, similar to Roman aqueducts and structures such as the Colosseum.

Trace the evolution of architecture from Greek through Roman, Romanesque, Gothic, Rennaissance, Georgian and Georgian Colonial. Colonial style architecture was and still is quite prevalent along the east coast. Along our southeastern coast, in the southwest, and along the western coast the Spanish Mission and Indian adobe style influenced the architectural design. Note that nearly every building in America, until the coming of the modern period, was directly influenced by one of these styles of architecture. Note how the Gothic style still persists even in newly built churches.

Encourage students to see the carvings and other ornaments over doors and windows and around balconies or cornices of many of our city buildings. Though interesting in themselves, many of them make unnecessary embellishments which do not add to the beauty of the total design. Modern architecture has eliminated them.

Have students collect clippings of modern architectural styles. Analyze these to discover what changes have developed and why. Note how the use of modern construction materials has provided opportunities for different types of structures. See how functionalism and simplicity have been stressed. Discuss exterior colors, and clean, simple design.

Other suggested activities

1. Find illustrations of buildings throughout the world which are typical of the country in which they are built.

2. Make a rendering of what is considered the most beautiful building in the community.

3. Design a facade of a modern building.

4. Make a model of an original building design.

5. Make a plaster model of some historical architectural detail.

6. Create a low relief architectural sculpture or mosaic design for a modern building.

7. Build a model of some famous building.

8. Redesign the front of some store in the area which is now poorly designed.

9. Draw plans and elevations for a suburban home.

10. Render the tower or some section of an interesting church in the community.

References

1. Moholy-Nagy, L., *The New Vision,* Geo. Wittenborn, Inc., New York, N. Y. 1947, p. 23.
2. Nicolaides, K. *The Natural Way to Draw,* Houghton Mifflin Co., Boston, Mass., 1941, Introduction.
3. Rannells, Edward W., *Art Education in the Junior High School,* Univ. of Kentucky, Lexington, Ky., 1946, pp. 92, 93.
4. Matisse, Henri, *The Nature of Creative Activity,* Education and Art, UNESCO, Paris, 1954, p. 21.
5. Courses of Study in Art Education, Bulletin 262, Dept. of Public Instruction, Harrisburg, Pa., 1951, p. 59.

Additional References

Color:
> Birren Faber, *Selling With Color,* McGraw-Hill Book Co., New York, N. Y., 1945.
> Cheskin, Louis, *Colors: What They Can Do For You,* Liveright Pub. Corp. Inc., 1949.
> Graves, Maitland, *The Art of Color and Design,* McGraw-Hill Book Co., New York, N. Y. 1941.

General:
> Faulkner and Others, *Art Today,* Henry Holt and Co., New York, N. Y., 1941.
> Kainz and Riley, *Exploring Art,* Harcourt, Brace and Co., New York, N. Y. 1948.
> Nicholas and Others, *Art for Young America,* Chas. A. Bennett Co., Inc., Peoria, Ill. 1952.
> Riley, Olive, *Your Art Heritage,* Harper Brothers, New York, N. Y. 1952.
> Simpson, Martha, *Art is for Everyone,* McGraw-Hill Book Co., New York, N. Y. 1951.
> Wickiser, Ralph L., *An Introduction to Art Activities,* Henry Holt & Co., New York, 1947.

Graphic:

Arnold, Grant, *Creative Lithography and How to Use It*, Harper and Bros., New York., N. Y., 1941.

Kautzky, Theodore, *Pencil Broadsides*, Reinhold Publishing Co., New York, N. Y., 1940.

Leighton, Claire, *Wood Engraving and Woodcuts*, Studio Press, New York, N. Y. 1945.

Loomis, Andrew, *Figure Drawing for All Its Worth*, Viking, New York 17, N. Y. 1943.

O'Hara, Elliot, *Making Watercolor Behave*, Putnam, New York 16, N. Y. 1932.

Shokler, Harry, *Artists Manual for Silk Screen Printing*, American Artists group, New York, N. Y. 1946.

Sternberg, Harry, *Modern Methods and Materials of Etching*, Mc-Graw-Hill Company, New York, N. Y. 1949.

Lettering:

Ballinger, Raymond, *Lettering Art in Modern Use*, Reinhold Publishing Co., New York, N. Y. 1952.

Eisenberg, James, *Commercial Art of Show Card Lettering*, D. Van Nostrand Co., Inc., 1945.

Make-up:

Corson, Richard, *Stage Make-Up*, F. S. Crofts and Co., New York, N. Y. 1942.

Perspective:

Lawson, Philip, *Practical Perspective Drawing*, McGraw-Hill Book Co., Inc., New York, 1943.

Posters:

Allner, W. H., *Posters*, Reinhold Publishing Co., New York, N. Y.

"The Walker." A first prize winner for persons under 14 in the National Soap Sculpture Contest. Soap provides an easily worked medium for an experience in sculpturing.

CHAPTER VII

DESIGNING WITH MATERIALS

O NLY for the sake of emphasis is this material on three-dimensional design treated here in a separate chapter. In no way should it be construed as something which may be "tacked on" to a regular course of study in art. It is an integral part of the course.

Visits to schools all over America have shown that most art programs place too much emphasis on drawing and painting. In many schools art is exclusively a two-dimensional experience. Books on art education have stressed two-dimensional art, with little or no discussion on three-dimensional. Some of the most

COURTESY OF THE SCULPTOR

The medium determines to a large extent the composition, technique, and final production. Complete respect for the medium is shown in this outstanding work by the sculptor Koren der Harootian. Permanent collection of the Pennsylvania Academy of Fine Arts.

PITTSBURGH PUBLIC SCHOOLS,
PITTSBURGH, PA.

Eighth grade students making papier mâché masks and animals. Can be used creatively in as many ways as the imagination allows.

3d + material

recent books on art education take this position. Ceramics is the most prevalent exception.

In America much of our environment is influenced by artists and designers. The tools and instruments that we use, vehicles we ride in, the rooms we relax and work in—even the views from our windows—are "designed" by someone.

Many of our fine artists now design with numerous materials other than conventional clay or stone. Modern man's creative expression is primarily in terms of *three dimensions* in an *almost unlimited* variety of materials.

If the art program is intended to develop a sense of appreciation for current art expression, considerable exploration and

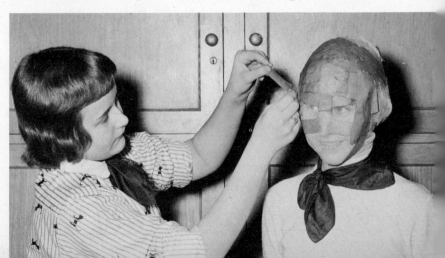

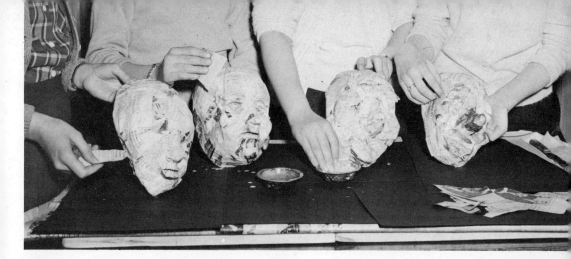

study has to be carried on in the area of three-dimensional design—designing with materials.

Never before has the creative mind of students been so challenged by such a wide variety of materials with which to create. Nor have they ever had such a broad selection of tools to use in the creating.

No longer does the production of an article begin and end with a mechanic. Almost everything that is produced today is styled from the very beginning by a designer. The buildings in which products are made, the machines which shape them, the trucks which transport them, the stores which sell them, the cases which display them, and the packages which contain them are all designed by artists. Our homes, our cars, our highways and landscapes, our bridges and our planes are

119

Materials can communicate directly with the student artist. This piece of driftwood suggested "Make me into a long ugly face."

all products from the designer's drawing board, as are the decorations and accessories in our homes, offices, and public buildings. An appreciation and understanding of all of this can be gained only by actual experience in three-dimensional expression with a variety of materials, tools and processes.

Pieces of wire, plastic, stone, clay, or wood come to life under the hands of the young artist. In turn the student's creative abilities are fired by the handling of the materials. Each material seems to speak a language all its own. Note how a youngster's hands begin to move when he holds a section or soft wire or clay. A youth picking up a piece of driftwood for study will handle it—feel it, turn it over, and familiarize himself with its natural structure "This piece of wood

120

Boys preparing clay which they themselves dug from pits which they discovered.

tells me to make a long ugly face," he decides. How different a reaction from that of students who have been handed paper and crayons with which to create. To some students the material seems to indicate the already existing sculptured form which is imprisoned and waiting liberation, as Michelangelo said, "by a process of removal."

Sensitive fingers and imagination are stimulated creatively by the contact with materials.

121

A study in form and

space created in clay.

Is it surprising that many of us find greater satisfaction in three-dimensional than in two-dimensional expression? Here, then, is a direct avenue of approach in developing art appreciation and stimulating creativity. If a student enjoys using tools and has a creative, inventive mind there is no limit to the exciting compositions which he can originate.

Certain materials lend themselves more readily to specific interpretations. So a variety of available materials is more likely to provide one or two uniquely adapted to some individual. A youngster who "doesn't know what to do with" colored sheets of plastic may feel completely at home with colored yarn and a frame loom. Another may create extensively in line by using copper wire, although he never reacted to the use of a pencil.

Many art educators and fine artists have been inclined to deplore as poor design some of the creations which are being sold. A society, trained in the schools which provides suitable background experience in the producing of aesthetically satisfactory designs in materials, will force the improvement of standards of all fine and commercial art productions.

Students who know how to design with materials will take their designs in to the shops to build. They will be more inclined to be critical and selective in their purchases.

There were few examples of creative expression in art in the past years which were not in the tradition of the Classic styles of Europe. The current expressions in three-dimensional design are primarily influenced by self expression as

122

determined by the variations and limitations of materials themselves.

A young doctor and an air force colonel were discussing the making of mobiles—an example of the "free" use of materials. When asked what prompted their attempts at creating in this style, they both replied with nearly the same answer: "I have no particular interest in art and never painted, nor thought that I could. Mobiles are a new expression; they are not confined by tradition; experimentation seems invited; personalized expression is called for. Also, there goes with it a challenge to man's manual dexterity and mechanical interest." Younger persons also welcome this challenge and freedom.

The traditional teaching of art, on all levels, was done to perfect techniques that led to a finished production. Very little emphasis was placed on creative compositions and experiments with materials in order to arrive at personal interpretations. In working with materials, the very nature of the media stimulates creative thinking and serves as a challenge to the individual.

There is much more flexibility in the use of materials than there is in working on a flat design with a graphic medium. Constant use of the pen and pencil for writing or figuring may tend to restrict our thinking when creating with these traditional tools on a flat surface. There are no such restrictive associations when we work with materials in three-dimensional design.

As has been previously pointed out, drawing is primarily visual whereas working with materials is more tactual. "Visual skills are reinforced by parallel tactual skills developed through the sensuous experience of materials and processes in evolving new forms. . . . Construction is realized in volumes and the hand is equally the source of sensation and the proof of rightness in the form evolved."[1]

Projects in this area should develop an appreciation for an "honest use of and respect for materials." The teacher must be alert to keep activities purposeful and to see that they do not develop into "busy work."

The term design has too often been interpreted as mean-

123

Pendants of this type, made of wood and silver, or all silver, are especially suited to junior high students as no soldering is required. The student is freed from the traditional limitations of the jewelry craft.

Using a hand vise to shape a wooden piece of a pendant on a wheel.

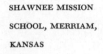

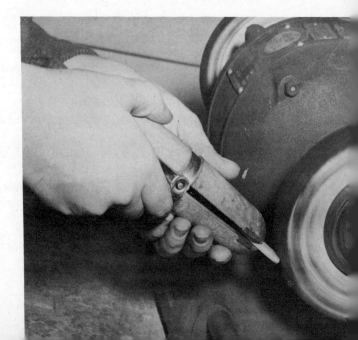

ing a decoration which has been applied to an object. Abstractions created in a variety of materials will enable students to appreciate that design is inherent in the creation and not something which is superimposed upon it.

As the projects are completed, point out the relationship between the principles of design indicated in student work and those same principles as observed in the professional work of sculptors, architects, and industrial designers. This does not mean a comparison of productive skill, which would be discouraging and would tend to influence the type of creations developed by the students.

Lack of materials need never be a deterrent. Many problems can be developed with inexpensive or scrap material. See the list in Chapter IX. Some materials which are indigenous to the particular area can be collected at little or no cost. Various projects can be successfully completed with a minimum amount of tools and equipment.

There is no sequence of problems in this field which can be definitely outlined. Following are listed a few projects in various materials. These will be easily integrated with the activities in two-dimensional expression which have been suggested in the preceding chapter. Work in the suggested areas and media will provide for considerable experimentation, creative expression, and application of design principles. There are many other problems which will be motivated through the natural interest of the students and the use of the materials themselves.

SUGGESTED ACTIVITIES

Wall designs

Use pieces of white cardboard to make a shallow-depth, abstract wall decoration. Corrugated board from old cartons can be used. The objective of this problem is to make the most interesting arrangement possible of simple shapes, suggesting depth, without the aid of color, textures, or values. Designs of this type are rather easy to develop as they are viewed only from the front. Later designs will be developed which can be viewed from all sides. The pieces of cardboard

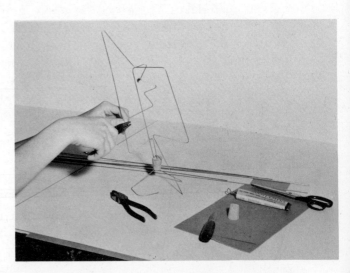

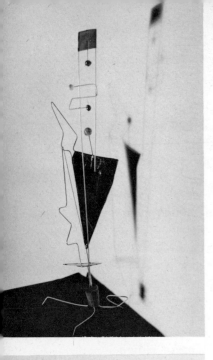

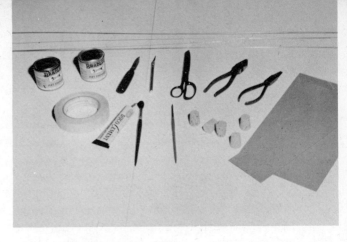

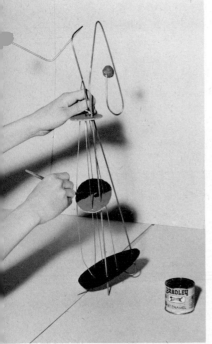

VALLEJO JUNIOR HIGH SCHOOL, VALLEJO, CALIF.

1. *Upper right: Materials needed for making simple stabiles in wire, cork and cardboard.*

2. *Lower right: A student shaping a stabile with the tools shown above.*

3. *Lower left: Painting the finished stabile.*

4. *Upper left: Finished stabile.*

are to be arranged so as to make an interesting vertical and horizontal pattern. The depth is created by using cardboard hinges to hold the separate pieces of the pattern at different distances from the background. Note how shadows can be

used for emphasis on certain parts. This problem can be followed by making similar compositions painted various values of gray, and black and white. This will show how tension, emphasis, and depth can be created by the use of strong contrasts in value. Also experiment with color, to see how it develops tensions and helps to establish emphasis and depth.

Now use various textured materials to create a design which combines color, value, line, mass, and texture. Some of the materials which can be included are: glass, wood, plastic, peg board, metal wire, screen, plaster, dowels, drawer pulls, thumbtacks, corks, and textiles. Airplane glue will secure these materials in place.

An interesting wall design can be made with a shallow box and yarn or string. Paint the interior of the box a color contrasting with the color of the yarn. Develop a line design by fastening the yarn to the inside of the four sides and the bottom of the box. The yarn can be brought out through holes in the box and fastened securely to the outside.

127

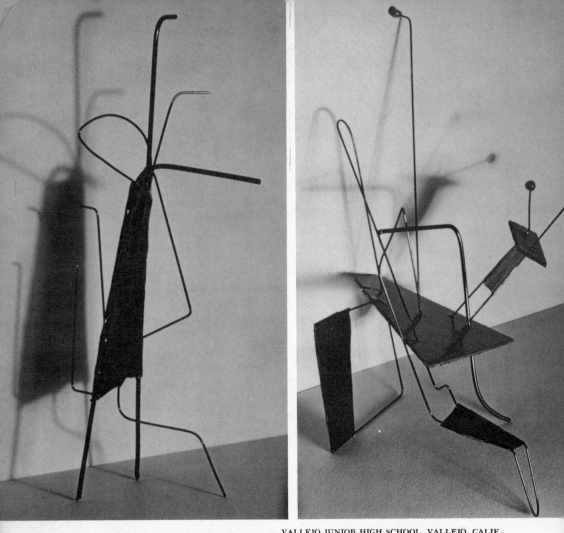

Stabiles present a challenge to the early adolescent in the study of form, color, space and the use of tools.

Stabiles or immobiles

Designing of stationary forms may profitably accompany the making of mobiles. Stabiles involve the same design principles as the making of wall designs, but with the additional problem of organizing forms which may be viewed from all sides. The experiences gained are of value in designing mobiles, which present the additional problem of movement in space.

A flat sheet of cardboard can be divided by lines into shapes which create an interesting two-dimensional design. Or

128

OAK PARK AND FOREST RIVER SCHOOL, OAK PARK, ILL.

Brayer print. Printers ink colors are freely spread out on a sheet of glass or aluminum. The brayer is rolled over this for one complete turn and then the ink is transferred to the paper from the brayer.

128A

NYACK JR.-SR. HIGH SCHOOL

A composition created with scraps of colored papers and old newspapers.

String painting done by drawing a paint loaded string out from between two pieces of paper. Surprisingly interesting results are obtained with this method even from those with the least talent.

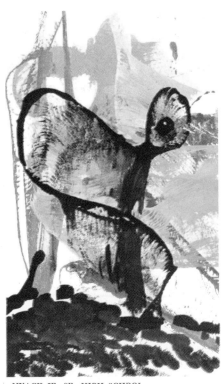

NYACK JR.-SR. HIGH SCHOOL

A *color interpretation inspired by contemporary dance music. Motivation by music encourages a free expression.*

NYACK JR.-SR. HIGH SCHOOL

128E

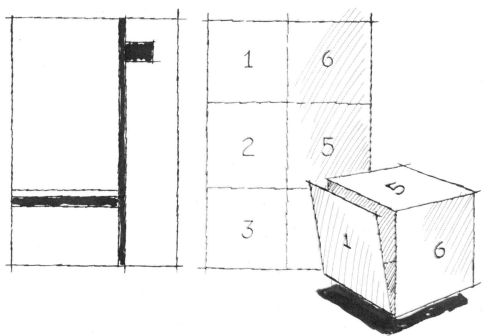

it can be divided and cut so that it creates a solid volume. Or it can be cut and arranged so that it creates the illusion of space. Use pieces of flat cardboard to create designs which emphasize space. Experiment with values and colors to see how they help to create interest in parts, develop tensions, and organize the whole. Fragment designs can be made, in which all parts cut from a single rectangle of cardboard are used in a composition. Stabiles can be developed using materials such as scrap pieces of wood, sheets of plastic, glass, wire screen, dowels, and other materials. Some students may

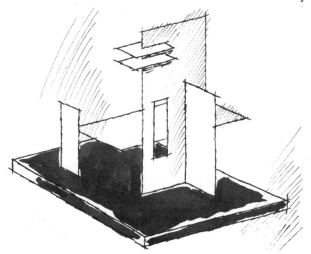

"Growth," a carving in plaster by an 8th grade girl. The roughly carved base contrasts effectively with the smoothly sanded upper part. Plaster is an easily carved and inexpensive medium.

want to develop a three-dimensional commercial display for some product, following the above experiments.

Experiment with line designs. Forms can be built with matches, toothpicks, or paper straws. These designs can also be effectively suspended.

The slim, rather stiff metal rods used in welding can be easily bent into rectangular shapes to make interesting stabiles. For the base, cut wood the desired size and drill holes the right diameter for the ends of rods, about 1/2 inch apart, in rows covering the base. Shape the rods before inserting.

Sculpture

After experiences with the preceding problems we are not so much inclined to think of sculpture in the traditional manner. We are ready to experiment with the materials and express our ideas in forms other than copies of nature. The student's wishes, the instructor's understanding, and the materials at hand will determine the approach to this unit and the extent to which it is developed. Many materials may be

130

Religious subject: This inexpensive and practical sculpturing medium for young adolescents was made from sawdust and plaster, cast into a shoe box. Black watercolor was added to give the material a stone gray effect. The medium can be carved, sawed, drilled, filed, and sanded. This incomplete piece shows the drill and saw marks.

used: copper and aluminum wire, "sculpt" stone, clay, plaster, "sculpt" metal, wood, stone, liquid and solid plastic, salt block, papier-mâché, sheet metal, and "styro" foam.

Plaster of Paris is a good, inexpensive, material, and commercial gauging plaster is even less expensive. It can be purchased in fifty pound bags. An excellent material for easy carving can be made by mixing gauging plaster with baking soda—ten parts of plaster to one part of soda. The material can be colored simply by adding dyes or airbrush paint to the wet mixture. Cast it in cardboard forms, and when set it is readily carved—even with a blunt knife or an orange stick.

Another interesting carving medium is made by mixing plaster with sawdust. This is also easily carved and gives the rough appearance of stone. If the material is to be colored, the sawdust should be colored before mixing it with the plaster.

Plaster can be used as a *modeling medium* if lime is added to the mixture to slow up the setting process. The plaster wall sculpture shown in illustration on page 25 was created with

131

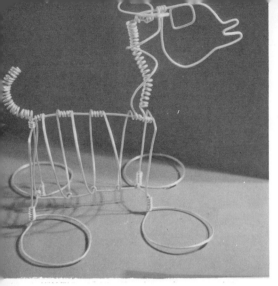

Animal sculpture done with aluminum clothes line wire. This is a pliable medium which stimulates creative thinking.

this medium. A variety of textures can be made on the surface, and it can be sanded, scraped, and cut.

Paper sculpture is inexpensive, and popular with most students. Impressive, large pieces can be created by using a wire or wood framework to support the paper. If sheet metal is available, some of the smaller articles can be made over into metal forms, using the paper pieces as patterns.

Flat pieces of papier-mâché can be built up with four or five layers of newspaper and paste. These sheets can then be cut with scissors and molded into any shape. When dry they

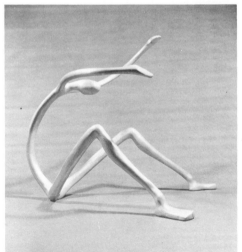

"The Tumbler," created by covering a solid wire armature with sculpt-metal—a plastic metal that hardens and can be filed and polished.

132

are very rigid, light, and can be easily painted. Cover with sculpt metal or liquid plastic to give a variety of textures.

Interpretations of animals, persons, or abstract figures can be formed by using a heavy-gauge *aluminum wire*. Wire cutters and pliers are about the only tools needed for this work. Light copper wire is very plastic and lends itself readily to the problem.

Boys will be interested in working with materials which call for the use of their maturing muscular strength. Wood, stone, and iron will challenge them. If a welding torch is available in the art studio or shops, fascinating pieces can be created in iron and in combinations of iron with wood or ceramics. Try salt blocks, used for feeding cattle. They come in several colors and sizes, and may be sawed, drilled, sanded, and chiseled. The salt can be softened for easier carving by moistening it with a wet sponge. NOTE: Care should be taken that students do not become discouraged in their efforts to create in these less pliable media.

Students will enjoy a visit to a local monument works to see how mechanics shape stone with both hand and power tools. Visit sculptors in the community. Arrange demonstrations and exhibits, if possible. There are some excellent films available on sculpturing.

Clay, of course, is an ideal medium for modeling. Firing clay can be used if permanent pieces are desired. Or "plasticene" can be used, and plaster casts made if a piece is to be preserved. Young persons enjoy the process. When dry, these pieces can be painted, varnished, and waxed in a variety of surface treatments.

NOTE: When plaster is used in the art studio, *extreme caution* should be exercised so that plaster does not get into the plumbing. Sinks should have clean-out traps. All wet plaster should be discarded into waste-buckets.

All tools and equipment must be immediately cleaned following use, as the plaster sets up very fast and does not move easily when hard.

Mobiles

These are designs moving in space. Probably no creation

is more attractive to the average person than a gracefully moving, well designed mobile. As modern mobiles have almost no history or tradition behind them, they invite exploration and experimentation.

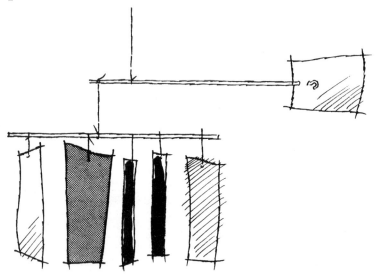

"Junk attached to wire."

Never lose sight of the fact that mobiles are problems in design. Too many mobiles are undesigned pieces of unrelated materials and shapes balanced on the ends of rods—junk attached to wire. Making a mobile requires a considerable amount of study and experimentation to develop balance, movement, and an organized design which is attractive in all positions.

The first experiments can be carried on with wire, thread, and cardboard. Use simple abstract shapes.

Cardboard parts. The balance point for each *piece* of any unit in the mobile can be determined by pushing a pin into the top edge of the cardboard at various places until the desired balance point is discovered. See Figure A, below. The pin can be left in and secured with a drop of airplane glue, or a hole can be punched at that point through which a thread can be run and tied. Nylon thread will support rather heavy

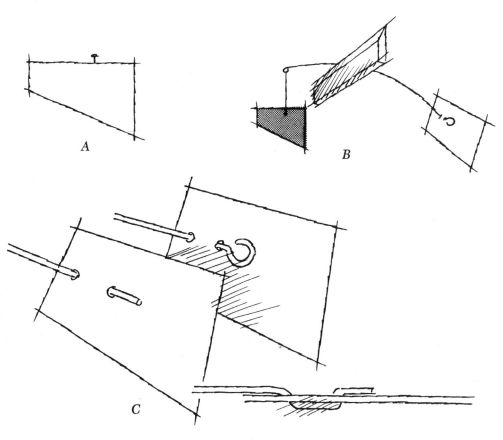

A

B

C

weights, has extremely free movement, and will last for an unbelievably long time.

The balance point of any completed *unit* in the mobile can be determined by testing it on the edge of a knife or a ruler. See Figure B. Then a loop in the wire can be made, or a thread secured at the point. Wrap the thread around the wire two or three times and fasten it with a drop of glue. Pieces which are to be immobile on the ends of arms can be fastened by gluing a loop of wire formed at the end of the arm to the flat piece. Or punch two holes in the flat piece and squeeze the wire flat after it has been run through the holes, as shown in Figure C.

Avoid formal balance for a dynamic, moving design. Designs can be made all black, or with areas of color or white.

135

The black mobiles are shown off to best advantage with a light background. If the design is to be hung in a dark place, light colors on the units will be necessary.

Many materials can be used for making mobiles, including thin sheets of glass, plastic and balsa wood, Christmas decorations, screens, metal foils, sheet metals, paper, and papier-mâché.

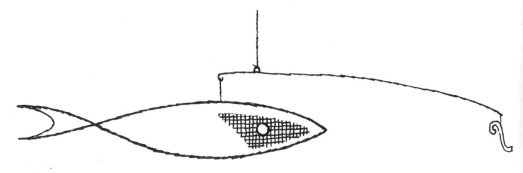

Wire parts. Use 12 to 18 gauge iron wire. Heavier gauges of aluminum wire can be easily bent to shape. Clothes-hanger

Pottery can be done with simplest of tools and equipment. All pieces shown here were done by the slab method, with the exception of the horse.

DENNIS JUNIOR HIGH SCHOOL, RICHMOND, IND.

Animals and figures in clay calls for personal interpretations.

wire and welding rods can be used for the stiff, supporting arms. However, they are too hard to bend when small loops are necessary.

Joints in the wire can be made solid by soldering when necessary, or they can be secured with fine wire, liquid solder, airplane glue, or thread and glue.

Making of mobiles is one of the most exciting problems in the art program. A generous display, throughout the school, of constantly moving, well designed mobiles is a proved means of promoting interest in the art program.

Ceramics

As has been pointed out, youngsters who are not inspired by two-dimensional projects often achieve success in designing with materials. This is especially true when working with plastic material such as clay.

All students should have some experiences in clay. In some communities clay can be dug at no cost. Small kilns

137

are not expensive. The gift of one of these might be arranged for through the local PTA, student council, or art club. All art programs should provide for activities in clay.

There are some excellent films on this subject which will help the student to understand the processes and techniques. To create a well-designed object out of a mass of clay, fire, and glaze, and complete it in its entirety, is a most gratifying creative experience.

If the art studio is not equipped with facilities for a full program in ceramics, then some limited experiences should be arranged. The coil and slab method could be used, if a wheel cannot be installed. Perhaps a kiln is available in the community where pieces could be fired. If possible, visit a kiln. Self-hardening clay can be used if firing is impossible. This clay can be painted with enamels to simulate glazes.

Demonstrate the making and use of press molds and slip molds. Discuss commercial pottery making. Show the methods of surface decoration, sgraffito, slip painting, and carving.

Study the various uses of ceramics today. Ceramics have made possible the development of jet engine aircraft, to insulate

Scrap cardboard is used to make looms for weaving. Old rags can be cut and used for the woof so that whole project can be done at almost no expense. The cardboard heddle speeds up the weaving and can be used on a wooden weaving frame also.
SHELBY PUBLIC SCHOOLS, SHELBY, N. C.

against the terriffic heat in the combustion chamber. Find the number of examples of ceramics in the home and school building.

Some schools, with superior programs in ceramics, engage a professional ceramist to supplement the work of the regular teachers once a week or so.

If ample equipment is available, extensive work in clay will hold the interest for long periods of time. There is so much to do and learn about ceramics. A lifetime hobby will begin for many students, because of their interest.

For many people there is no other craft which is so exciting to watch as that of an accomplished potter throwing a vase on a wheel. Some cannot engage in this process without feeling a kinship with God. Literally, by a mere pressure of the fingers, a beautiful, useful object grows, in minutes, out of a chunk of raw earth. No wonder our Creator has been referred to in prose and poetry as the Great Potter.

Weaving

Though weaving is generally thought of as two-dimensional, it is included here because so many kinds and combinations of materials can be used.

Weaving is one of the most primitive, and essential, of all crafts. Imagine the difference in our dress if weaving were not possible. It can be carried on with the simplest of handmade equipment and with readily available materials.

Provide for each student to weave at least one small piece of material. A handmade loom, string, and strips of old cloth can be used.

Practical place mats can be made from almost any fiber. Some of these are: grapevines, rattan, raffia, grasses, corn husks, alder and lilac shoots, cattails, golden rod canes, bamboo, rags, forsythia, pine needles, willow twigs, rushes, ropes, and ash strips. By varying the colors of the warp threads, interesting designs can be created. Some dyed weft material can be used also. Inexpensive rug yarns provide a wide range of colors. If treadle looms are available then the design possibilities are almost unlimited.

Some useful articles which can be woven with simple

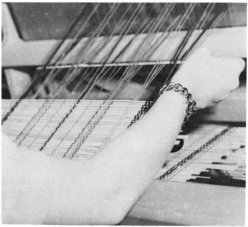

The weaving of bamboo table place mats and centerpieces is especially appealing to junior high students. A mat can be completed in a few minutes after the loom has been warped. A variety of colors has been introduced here in the warp threads.

equipment in the studio classroom are: hot dish mats, scarves, tables runners, wrap-around skirts, hand bags, ties, chair covers, lamp shades, rugs, porch screens, decorative house screens, pot holders.

Have students list as many uses of textiles as possible. These include: clothing, draperies, carpets, wall coverings, luggage, window screens, upholstery covers, shoes, hosiery, bandages and many others.

If time permits experiment with natural dye materials such as: butternuts, onion skins, lily-of-the-valley leaves sumac, sunflower seeds, and golden rod.

Discuss the source and preparation of such materials for weaving as wool, cotton, linen, and synthetic yarns. Experiment with carding (combing) and spinning wool or cotton into yarn. Collect samples of the many ways that textiles are decorated. Include printing, dyeing, appliqué, stenciling, and embroidery.

Other suggestions

Make use of materials which are indigenous to the area

140

in which the students live. Those who live near the ocean, lakes, or rivers will be able to secure *driftwood* which will serve as a challenging material to sculpture or to develop into useful articles such as lamp bases. *Cypress knees* in the southern states also offer a most stimulating material with which to create.

City areas provide an abundance of material from its many factories and assembly plants. Most business houses are co-operative in supplying waste or damaged materials to the schools at little or no cost. One metropolitan instructor has a large room filled with several thousand dollars worth of woods, metals and plastics which has been given to him by local firms for his creative craft program. Another instructor has developed contacts with two different concerns which supply him with leather ends for use in bookbinding, without even the cost of postage, though they are sent several hundred miles.

Beaches, brook beds, and deserts will provide beautiful stones which can be polished and made into *jewelry*. Shells of many kinds can also be collected and made into many useful and decorative articles.

Where special *native crafts* have persisted or been re-vived, make use of this natural interest in the community. Bring in the local craftsmen to demonstrate and exhibit. If possible have them teach units of work in their particular field.

Some localities have "old-country" groups which desire to carry on with their native crafts. Help develop this in-terest among the young generation.

In rural and suburban communities, make use of the abundance of seasonal flowers and plant life to develop a unit in *floral arrangement* and *gardening*. This project calls for a considerable amount of initiative. Have members of local garden clubs come in for demonstrations and slide talks.

Novelty jewelry, made of all sorts of materials, can be carried on with little or no expense. Use combinations of such materials as wire, rivets, bolts, nails, nuts, washers, and cotter pins. These can be attached to jewelry findings with liquid solder or ambroid cement to make pins and earrings. The

141

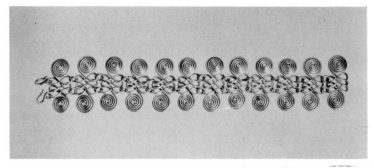

HANDY HARMON COMPANY

A wire bracelet made without any soldering. A simple bending jig was made by driving nails into a block of wood. Each unit was made separately and fastened together with links.

A sterling silver pin made by bending wire around nails driven into a board in the pattern desired. No soldering is necessary.

young fry will love these. Wire pins and bracelets can be made without solder or any equipment except round and square nosed pliers.

Tin cans will supply material for many projects.

INDUSTRIAL DESIGN

Industrial design is a relatively new field. By and large, teacher training institutions have not emphasized its importance in the art curriculum. It is essential that the art course be arranged to develop an understanding and appreciation of

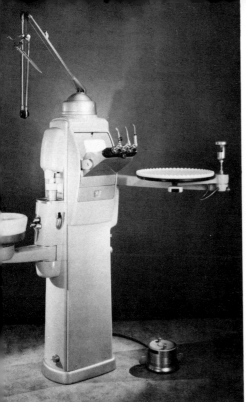
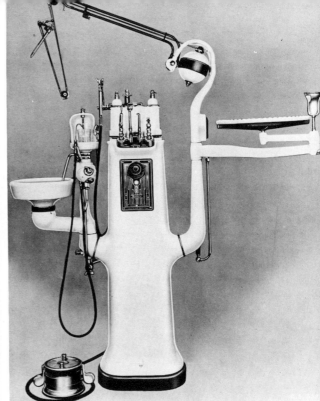

A new and an old design for a dental unit.

this form of artistic expression, which is so prevalent and with which we are almost steadily in contact. Industrial design covers everything—as Raymond Loewy subtitles his personal record—"from lipsticks to locomotives."

Their experiences with material designs will help students to appreciate some of the problems involved in industrial designing. Too often critics of the industrial designer are not aware of the problems with which he contends. He has to make a design that is fresh yet not radical, with the most practical material, as aesthetically beautiful as possible, and still functional. He also is obliged to design a product which appeals to the aesthetic level of every potential consumer.

Raymond Loewy comments: "It is a proven fact that there is as yet no general acceptance of products whose design has been reduced to their simplest expression outside of a limited segment of sophisticated buyers, representing perhaps a few per cent of the consuming public."[2]

The top designer is always conscious of the need for simple beauty in his creations. However, production methods,

143

WALTER DORWIN TEASE ASSOCIATES

function, cost, tradition, and materials have to be considered in his designs. "Design today as always is directed by the interplay of materials, methods and functions, with forms determined by materials as much as by function."[3]

"As the designer succeeds in organizing a product as nearly as possible in its ultimate *right* form, he also succeeds in revealing to the speculative eye of a purchaser, the values and merits which have actually been built into it in the course

144

of its painstaking engineering. He is approximating in the mechanical realm, what nature does when she impresses upon us the beauty of an all-around athlete's body or the rippling high-lights in a fine horse's well groomed coat. If he succeeds in achieving an evident rightness he makes a powerful appeal to our strongest aesthetic responses."[4]

The fine artist, working in three dimensions, has only to select his theme and materials, and then has free rein in making a composition as aesthetically perfect as possible to state his message. The materials themselves set up the primary limitations; the result does not have to be functional, pour easily, run smoothly, withstand constant operation, or sell to a large segment of the public.

The industrial designer is more than a creator of sleek streamlined covers for machines. "He is at once an artist, visionary, a practical planner, a technician and business man, working in a highly volatile field whose requirements and needs change from day to day."[5]

Usually, in the past, the young student with a creative mind and interest in building things has been directed away from art into the field of engineering. Industrial designing offers a challenging opportunity to combine artistic talent and practical creativeness into a superb professional career. The leading art colleges report their inability to fill all the requests for industrial design graduates.

Emergence of industrial design

As the industrial revolution developed and machines became more prevalent, they also became more clumsy and bulky. Gadgets were added to them as needed. At first, no matter how they looked, if the machines worked they were good. Then gradually these bulky monstrosities became decorated with sunset scenes, garlands of roses, and cast-iron grapevines—superimposed nonsense in the worst of the Beauxarts tradition.

With the advent of the industrial designer, styling was built into the machine and its products. The engineer and the industrial designer worked together to make everything more compact and graceful, and actually improve it function-

145

ally. Sloping lines, given such names as "tumblehome" or "accelerated perspective," which tend to add grace and functional expression to objects, have almost completely replaced the bulky, awkward lines of the past. The machine tools behind this amazing economics revolution have been given beauty, dignity, color, and grace by the industrial designer. Better use of old and new materials, and quantity production methods, help make low-priced, beautiful products feasible.

Discuss with the students the many steps a designer must take in the development of a final product. These include—after and during consultation with management, engineers, and the sales force—sketches, renderings, clay models, plaster models, full size experimental models, color schemes, working drawings, and many other intermediate and repeat details. The finished product is the result of the *team effort* of a large number of remarkable persons.

Suggested activities

1. Design a cosmetic bottle. Make sketches of it and model it in clay.

2. Make a wood model of an airplane. Finish it as smoothly as possible and paint it with enamel or aluminum.

3. Make a small model of an automobile. Work from sketches and build the model of plastic material. If time permits cast the model in plaster and paint it.

4. Make elevation drawings for a television cabinet or a home freezer. Do a color rendering.

5. Sketch or model a flat iron or toaster. Cast it in plaster and paint it with aluminum paint and black or colored enamel.

6. Use wire and balsa wood to make a model of a "wrought iron" chair.

7. Design and make a cardboard model of a dressing table.

8. Select an article which you feel is poorly designed and redesign it.

9. Design a package for a tube of toothpaste.

10. Make working drawings for a simple piece of wrought iron furniture which is to be built in the school shop.

References

1. Rannells, Edward W., *Art Education in the Junior High School,* University of Kentucky, Lexington, Ky., 1946, p. 114.
2. Loewy, Raymond, *Never Leave Well Enough Alone,* Simon and Schuster, Inc., New York, N. Y., 1951, p. 222.
3. Teague, Walter D., *Design This Day,* Harcourt, Brace & Co., Inc., 1940, New York, N. Y., p. 69.
4. Teague, Walter D., *The Field of Industrial Design,* 1954, March & April, Design Magazine, Columbus, Ohio, p. 172.
5. Immermann, Milton, *A Career for You in Industrial Design,* 1954, March & April, Design Magazine, Columbus, Ohio, p. 173.

Additional References

Architecture:
  Bitterman, Eleanor, *Art in Modern Architecture,* Reinhold Publishing Corp., New York, N. Y.
Ceramics:
  Janeway, Carol, *Ceramic and Pottery Making for Everyone,* Tudor Publishing Co., New York, N. Y., 1950.
  Kenny, John, *Ceramic Sculpture,* Greenberg Publisher.
Enameling:
  Bates, Kenneth, Enameling, *Principles and Practice,* The World Publishing Co., Cleveland and New York, 1951.
Flower Arrangement:
  Rockwell, Frederick, *Complete Book of Flower Arrangement,* American Garden Guild, New York, N. Y., 1947.
General:
  Tomlinson, R. R., *Crafts for Children,* Studio Publications Inc., New York, N. Y., 1935.
Jewelry:
  Mortin and D'Amico, *How to Make Modern Jewelry,* Museum of Modern Art and Simon and Schuster (Distributors), New York, N. Y., 1949.
  Winebrenner, D. Kenneth, *Jewelry Making,* International Textbook, Scranton, Pa., 1953.
Marionettes:
  Beaton and Beaton, *Marionettes; a Hobby for Everyone,* Crowell, New York, N. Y., 1948.
Mobiles:
  Lynch, John, *How to Make Mobiles,* Studio-Crowell, New York, N. Y., 1954.
Paper Sculpture:
  Johnston, Mary Grace, *Paper Sculpture,* The Davis Press, Worcester, Mass., 1952.

Miller, J. V., *Paper Sculpture and Construction*, C. A. Bennett, Peoria, Ill., 1957.

Plastics:

Robinson, Clark, *Meet the Plastics*, Macmillan Co., New York, N. Y., 1949.

Puppets:

Batchelder, Marjorie, *The Puppet Theatre Handbook*, Harper and Bros., New York, N. Y., 1947.

Weaving:

Brown, Harriet, *Hand Weaving for Pleasure and Profit*, Harper and Bros., New York, N. Y., 1952.

Gallinger and Benson, *Hand Weaving with Reeds and Fibers*, Pitman, 1948.

CHAPTER VIII   COUNSELING

URING the junior high years the "coin is in the air," and when it lands almost every interested student will have decided for or against a career in art. The vitality and challenge of his art experiences and his rapport with the art teacher will be important if not determining factors in the decision which he makes.

Counseling is of utmost significance at this stage of development. Unfortunately, it is a part of teacher preparation which is often neglected.

Many phases of pupil guidance can be carried on as well or better by other guidance specialists in the school organization as by individual teachers. However, helping a talented art student assimilate adequate information and acquire the proper attitude for making decisions about his career is a job which is *best done by the art teacher.*

(1) He is in close contact with the students while they struggle through the creative processes. (2) He is able to recognize the variations of abilities and interests. (3) He can supply the necessary informative literature when it will be most effective. (4) He knows of the specialized qualities necessary for success in the art occupations. (5) He can better recognize talent and, most important of all, the ability to apply it—even when it is laborious. (6) The art teacher is the most logical person to counsel on vocational art education.

A superintendent of schools writes in *The Nation's Schools:* "Counseling should no longer be considered apart from but

149

a part of the junior high curriculum. It should be as important to meet the need of the adolescent for emotional adjustment as for algebraic proficiency. Unless it is planned, counseling becomes incidental and often superficial."[1]

Many adjustments to school, home, and social life have to be made by the early adolescent. Often these adjustments are not easy ones. Art interest ofttimes is the one means of "getting to" the student who needs assistance. Then the art teacher can be more effective as a counselor than any other staff member. Sometimes success in the creative arts is the factor needed to help establish a sense of security.

Efficient counseling demands a daily contact with the young person—to know his aims, ambitions, abilities, special interests, limitations, background, and the conflicts peculiar to this age level. Home visits are often of immeasurable importance. Knowing the student will enable the teacher to set up real challenges for the competent and/or gifted person and to make proper allowances for others.

Vocational art counseling

Several *art tests* are used by vocational counseling services. They measure factors such as art appreciation, design sense, and taste or reaction to design elements. But they can serve only as possible clues to abilities or potentialities. The extent to which valid testing of this sort can be carried on is still being explored. The reaction of a student to an isolated design element, and to a production including a combination of several elements, is a very different matter. Evaluation of active participation in the creative process is also rather difficult. Scores from tests can be used only as an additional tool in formulating plans by the counselor. However, the results sometimes indicate special abilities in particular areas. It is important that the art teacher familiarize himself with such tests if they are used by his school system in order that he may intelligently interpret their significance to the students, parents, and other teachers.

Parents often consult the art teacher for advice, usually when they feel their child has exceptional ability that should be developed.

150

Virtually all guidance authorities say we should encourage even a genius to participate fully in the school art program and to carry on a vigorous, normal, healthy life with his age-mates during after-school hours. If he is to become an artist, no harm will be done by delaying his specialized training in art until after secondary school graduation. On the other hand, considerable harm can result from ill-directed art experiences in the formative years.

If parents *and the youth himself* are determined to secure extra instruction, help them to enroll him in the classes of a competent artist-teacher who will stick to the basic principles of exploring the art forms. Some private teachers and museums carry on worth-while classes in the arts.

Beware the "fine art" specialist, who is more dangerous than the commercial hack. Often he is a frustrated, semi-successful fine artist with no training or experience in pedagogy. There is a risk that training under such an instructor will do more harm than good. Some of these art teachers have an engaging personality and aesthetic mannerisms which intrigue parents. What are the artist's educational background, experience, qualifications? Is he truly an art educator or is he a businessman using art education as a commodity? Will he develop the natural creative ability or will he *project his own style* and please the parents by allowing Johnny to sign his name to a teacher painting, which is to be brought home and hung in the living room for all to admire? Too often these artists develop nothing but bad replicas of themselves.

The job of the counselor is to *provide the information and background* which will enable the student to make a wise choice of a vocation. *It is not to direct the selection of a choice.* When it is evident that a student lacks the qualifications for success in vocational art, the teacher should suggest as many other vocational opportunities as possible in other areas.

Supply as much vocational literature as possible for the students and parents. Bring in art professionals to discuss their vocations. Acquaint students with art vocations while creative problems are being developed. Integrate guidance with the art course.

The following was written especially for this chapter by

151

Mr. Leonard Miller, Chief Specialist in Guidance, United States Office of Education:

The art teacher, without extensive formalized preparation in guidance methods and techniques, can provide the following specific guidance services.

1. Be willing to follow suggestions from specialists for improving any classroom practices which may help the pupil toward self adjustment.
2. Look for interest patterns and encourage pupils to explore career opportunities.
3. Keep an open file of career information and refer pupils to source material in the library.
4. Show career films; display pamphlets, articles, and posters on bulletin boards.
5. Acquaint pupils with fields of work and leisure time activities for which a background in art has significance.
6. Administer or recommend the use of achievement, interest and/or aptitude tests which may add some helpful clues to junior high school pupils in their choice of and preparation for a career.
7. Invite various types of artists to meet with the art classes and talk about opportunities and preparation required in their respective fields.
8. Visit places in the community where pupils can observe workers employed in art and related fields.
9. Prepare and conduct assembly programs in which careers in art and related fields are portrayed.
10. Plan and conduct clubs which will provide special activities for pupils with art interests.
11. Observe behavior patterns—the effects of any physical or mental handicaps of a pupil on his classroom work or his relationship with other pupils.
12. Be alert to make referrals to specialists on the staff when the pupils' problems are too difficult for the teacher to handle.
13. Utilize cadet teachers as extensively as possible, not only to acquaint prospective teachers with the opportunities and responsibilities of art teachers but to involve these cadets as much as feasible in the guidance aspects of the art teachers' program as described above.

Success in the arts calls for drive, energy, ability, personality, business acumen, and personal sacrifice. Highly publicized success stories of bizarre personalities, with emphasis on other than the salient facts of success, have led many to interpret an art career as a glamorous profession which pays fantastic compensation for the most easily created productions.

152

Quality of success

Success in the *fine arts*, in almost every instance, demands great sacrifice, considerable privation, and an almost dedicated life—although this does not mean that the fine artist is a beret-wearing Bohemian, living in a garret and subsisting on wine and crackers. *Commercial art* also requires tremendous concentration, dedication, a high degree of trained talent, and the ability to meet strong competition. The commercial artist usually begins at a very low salary and gradually works up, if his ability warrants it.

The will to persevere and overcome all impediments is a most important character trait in the successful artist. Certainly a large dash of natural talent is no insurance of success. Case histories include many young people who have shown great promise in art schools but have failed in the competitive world because of lack of drive and integrated personalities. Others, with the bare minimum of natural flair, have succeeded financially in the art field because they were filled with drive. They forced success. Matisse was quoted earlier in the book as saying that the genuine creator is not just a gifted being but one who has the personality and ability to organize and express his concepts. This is true in any art expression.

An article in the *American Artist* magazine about silver-smiths states some very pertinent facts which can be applied to any branch of commercial art: "The building of such careers involves something beyond great talent. The fashioning of intractable materials, however beautiful, demands native constructive ability and perfect coordination of mind, eye and hand. And without patience and energy beyond the usual conception of physical effort, the goal is elusive. Not only that; learning how to adjust one's self and one's work to the market, no matter how specialized, takes years of constant study and effort—sometimes heart break too."[2]

The intent here is not to overemphasize the difficulties in commercial art but to try to strip it of its artificial glamour. The personal satisfactions of working in the art field are many and gratifying. For the person who is properly equipped, a profession in the commercial arts is a most pleasant way of earning a living.

153

The financial returns are worth seeking. Top designers and artists, of course, earn up to $30,000 and $40,000 a year. But there are also many opportunities in modest fields. For instance, a person who can do top-notch lettering, layout, or practical agency design, can earn considerably more than the average salaried worker.

Cartooning is probably one of the most misunderstood of all phases of commercial art. Many youngsters seem to think that no training in art is necessary for success in this field. They would do well to read *Careers in Cartooning*, by Lawrence Lariar. He says: "These eager enthusiasts are composed, for the most part, of optimists who imagine that cartooning is an easy craft, to be learned at their leisure. They are quite sure that a cartoon is nothing more than a 'trick' drawing and are convinced that they too will be able to sell comics once these 'tricks' have been mastered."[3] Like all other areas, cartooning requires specialization. Most advertising artists could not do a successful cartoon. This is true of other branches of commercial art. General art talent does not insure success in any specialty chosen at random. The student must select a branch for which he is uniquely suited, and then develop his natural talent through many years of continuous training and struggles.

The field of animated cartooning offers real opportunities. Newspapers employ local cartoonists. Television uses cartoonists all over the country. Most cartoon drawings in magazines are done on a free-lance basis. Comic strips are syndicated on a national basis.

Church art, which has not been remunerative for the artist, is fast developing since the war. In 1955 nearly five thousand new church buildings were erected in America. Nearly eighty million dollars worth of woodcarvings, wrought iron and stained glasswork, sculptures, and mosaics were created by artists and artist-craftsmen. The church has again become a patron of the arts.

Art directing is a complex, important job in commercial art. The art director coordinates many details in an advertising agency preparing displays for newspapers, magazines, shop counters and windows, signboards, television, or radio. Under

154

Ethel Waters

An example of a high form of the cartoonist's art. A caricature of the nightclub singer, Ethel Waters, arranged into a decorative design. Drawing originally appeared in drama section of the New York Times.

his direction work the idea men, sketch artists, photographers, typographers, illustrators, draftsmen, and layout men. His is a very responsible and strenuous position. Seeing that a large group of individuals complete their specialized jobs in time to compose the results and meet deadlines over a period of a few years burns out all but the most durable. Art directing is a position to which advertising artists, and others, rise through several years of experience in an advertising agency. One must know a considerable amount about all phases of art and copy production, sales techniques, business methods, and

155

media, including every new use of materials that occurs.

In addition to advertising agencies, art directors are employed by entertainment producers, manufacturers, publishers, printing houses, sign companies, and department stores. Salaries run from about $5,000 to $30,000 and more.

Illustration is an import segment of commercial art. The illustrator must be an excellent draftsman, proficient in one or two techniques, but generally he specializes in one particular area. He may do fashions, sports, historical scenes, humorous illustrations, etc. Others specialize in rendering products such as automobiles, tractors, heavy equipment, or even automobile tires. Or they can supply illustrations for specific types of magazines such as hobby crafts, sports, pulps, technical, religious, or business trades. Illustrators work both free-lance and in the employ of magazines, manufacturers, agencies, and art services. Incomes range from about $3,000 to $25,000 and higher.

Industrial design has been discussed in the preceding chapter. As in other coordinating posts, ability to get along with people is as important as talent. The productions of the industrial designer are the results of teamwork. The work of the industrial designer consists of three elements—design, merchandising, and engineering. There are ever-increasing opportunities in the field. The average income is high.

Advertising artists may work for business houses in merchandising, for advertising agencies, for art services, or free-lance. Business houses hire artists to style their products, design displays, decorate windows, etc. Jobs are open in lettering, decorating, and package designing.

Interior decoration as a profession has been affected by the trend away from large houses and period furniture. However, more decorators are being employed to decorate hotels, bars, shops, and offices, and to assist in the merchandising of home furnishings.

Textile designing is done for one of the largest industries in America. Salaries for top designers are high. They must have a knowledge of the industry, and weaving and printing processes. Most designers are trained in art schools. This is one of the commercial art fields which offer opportunities

156

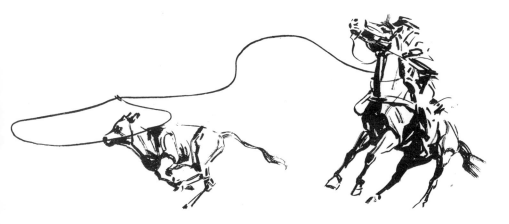

MC GRAW-HILL BOOK COMPANY

Expressive illustrations of animals demands that the artist be thoroughly familiar with his subject and have the technical craftsmanship to render them in all of their many actions. Illustration by Pres Crowell, from Cavalcade of American Horses.

for women. Much of the work is done on a free-lance basis. There are design rendering jobs in textiles for people who are not especially talented but who are sensitive to color and can handle a brush well.

Other opportunities in commercial art include interior design, ceramics, furniture design, landscape architecture, museum work, wallpaper design, stage design, costume design, fashion illustration, jewelry design, graphic arts, greeting card design, weaving, and all the crafts.

Fine artists find themselves, by and large, in a financially precarious profession. Income is very indefinite and irregular. If one feels that the only way his message can be presented to the world is through a career in fine art, it is best to have a rich and generous uncle. Even the most successful artists find it necessary sometimes, if not continually, to supplement their income by teaching or other work. If the fine artist is willing to meet the demands of the commercial world he can sometimes create for commercial advertising or do book illustrations. Sculptors find commissions rather difficult to procure. Some commissions pay well but come in very seldom. Mural

157

painting seems to have lost ground. High building costs may have cut down on the amount of money left for murals. Portrait painting can be made to pay if the artist has the skill to render likenesses and induce a steady flow of patrons. Unless a student has a *burning desire to be a fine artist* and is willing to look forward realistically to life which promises little or no security, or unless he has a private income, he should not be encouraged to embark on a fine art career. Usually those individuals who have the characteristics of the true artist will go ahead with their careers regardless of any advice or obstacles.

Teaching art is a career which is not, and probably won't be, overcrowded for many years to come. The art teacher can do a real service to art education by encouraging able, talented, and personable young people to consider teaching as a profession. Income, opportunities, and qualifications are well known in the profession. Salaries currently range from about $2,500 for beginners in some localities to a maximum of $9,300 in a few areas.

Avocational art holds interest for many people even though their careers are in other fields. There is a steadily increasing group of art hobbyists in the many branches of creative expression. Adult education classes offer inexpensive or free instruction for many of these people. Most communities of any size have art organizations which have been formed to further the fellowship and interest of members. There are professional fine artists who conduct classes for the art hobbyist. The Amateur Artists Association of America, Inc., has grown out of the national interest in the amateurs' section in the *American Artist* magazine. Many museums sponsor art classes for those who desire to carry on their interest on an avocational basis.

References

1. Eldredge, H. D., *Junior High Schools or High Schools for Juniors,* Article in The Nations Schools, June 1953, p. 74.
2. Winter, Edward, *3 American Silver Smiths,* Article in American Artist Magazine, May 1953, p. 30.
3. Lariar, Lawrence, *Careers in Cartooning,* Dodd, Mead & Co., New York, N. Y., 1950, Copyright © 1950 by Lawrence Lariar, p. 1.

Teacher References

1. Davis, Frank G. and Norris, Pearl S., *Guidance Handbook for Teacher*, McGraw Hill Book Co., New York, N. Y., 1949.

    For the teacher with a limited background in educational guidance.

2. Greenleaf, Walter J., *Occupations and Careers*, McGraw Hill Book Co., New York, N. Y. 1955.

    Information on all careers with a section on art. Latest listings of opportunities in art. Excellent book for the teacher for general guidance.

Student References

1. Biegeleisen, Jacob Israel, *Careers in Commercial Art*, Dutton and Company, 1952.

    Information on art in television and the various careers in art and relation to industry.

2. Gilbert, Dorothy, Editor, *American Art Directory*, R. R. Bowker Co., 1952.

    Lists the schools, colleges and universities in the United States, Canada and Latin America offering studies in art. Gives complete information on training for the fine arts.

3. Institute of Research, *Art as a Career*.

    Gives facts to help student decide about an art career, describes training, qualifications, salaries and related careers.

4. McCausland and others, *Art Professions in the United States*, Cooper Union Art School, New York, N. Y. 1950.

    Lists occupations, current trends, salaries. Report on survey of the alumni of the art school.

5. Price, Matlack, *So You're Going to be an Artist*, Watson-Guptill Publications Inc., New York, N. Y. 1946.

    Offers many helpful hints on how to prepare and to sell one's self as an artist.

6. Rochester Institute of Technology, *Careers in the Crafts*, 1953. Rochester, N. Y.

    Free booklet describing the hand crafts. Information on abilities needed and vocational opportunities.

CHAPTER IX SUPPLIES, BUDGET, AND FACILITIES

A WIDE variety of materials, tools, and equipment in the art course tends to broaden its scope and facilitate the structuring of each problem. Having equipment and materials available calls for intelligent advance planning by the art teacher.

Acquiring tools and equipment, and planning facilities, does not always fall to his lot. However, ordering supplies is generally the teacher's responsibility. Even this may baffle and frighten the inexperienced, the newly appointed person. Yet there are certain few procedures which will assist him, and which will indicate to the administration that all his work will be done efficiently.

The following valuable advice was written for this chapter by Mr. George Grice, an art supply house representative with many years experience in trying to decipher art teachers' supply orders. It is adapted from lectures prepared for college art education majors.

Making out an art supply requisition

What you get and how much is paid for material usually depends largely upon how well the requisition is executed. Thus the requisition is a very important part of art teaching. First take a complete inventory of all art materials. Next make a list of the various projects planned for the year. The third step is to write down everything you might possibly need to carry out the program.

All of this data must be set down on a form of some kind. Some schools have a standard form which the teacher is re-

quired to use. The form suggested below will prove helpful.

Description	Total Amount Needed	On Hand	Amount To Order	Estimated Cost & Special Remarks
(6″)	(2″)	(2″)	(2″)	(6″)

Use a sheet of 12″ x 18″ smooth white drawing paper and divide the paper into five columns, with the paper in a horizontal position. The first column at the left of the paper should be 6 inches wide, with the next three 2 inches wide. The last one will also be 6 inches wide. Proceed as follows: from the "Total amount needed" subtract the "on hand" figure and the result obtained will be the figure you need "To order." Thus if you need 50 packages of green paper a year and you have "On hand" 10 packages, the "Amount to order" would be 40 packages.

Now comes the most important part of all—describing or specifying the materials wanted. The best source of information is from a complete school supply house catalog. It is best to have several such catalogs if possible. Always list the brand name, style number, manufacturer's name, size or packing, name of supply house where goods can be purchased, and the estimated cost. It is a great help for the teacher to keep a special file of circulars, catalogs, samples, and any other information picked up at conferences, conventions, workshops, or by personal contact with the many representatives from supply houses. Do not hesitate to write for color charts and sample materials in which you have interest. Manufacturers and distributors are happy to furnish them. Experience shows that it is best to ask for material by a definite brand name—not just "poster paint" etc. This indicates the definite quality which is desired. Suppliers who may not stock this brand will then offer alternate items in the same classification. If the brand ordered is a second quality line, the substituted items will be second quality also. Remember price represents only what you pay, quality represents the value received. For

161

some projects the top grade material is not necessary or advisable. In other cases the top grade will be most economical.

Avoid the use of general terms such as "boxes of coloring crayons." This request may be interpreted as wax crayons, pressed crayons, chalk crayons, wax-pressed crayons, graphite crayons, and could be wrapped or unwrapped, full length, round, square, hexagonal, flat, or half round. They could be in cardboard boxes with tuck ends, lift lid, hinged, telescope top, metal box, wooden box, or plastic boxes. The diameter could be anywhere from $\frac{1}{4}''$ to one inch. There are assortments of 6, 8, 12, 16, 20, 24, 32, 36, 48, 54, and 60 to a box. In addition there are a dozen different manufacturers of crayons. This is not an isolated item. Some could be interpreted in even more ways. Accordingly, specify definitely as to what is wanted.

When ordering papers, mention weight in pounds, such as 56 lb. manila drawing. Do not use terms such as "light," "medium," or "heavy," unless accompanied by a weight. Satisfactory white drawing papers should be a minimum of 60 lb. For average work 70 lb. is a better weight. Eighty pound might be termed medium and matches the weight of good construction paper. Water color papers are usually 90 to 100 lb. weight as are white papers for pen and ink or mechanical drawing. A description and the weight is given in all reliable school supply company catalogs. From experience and/or trying samples a teacher soon learns the type of paper that does the job best and for the least expense. The economy of quality should never be overlooked.

The companies specializing in materials for schools offer the widest and most complete range of materials in regard to both price and choice. Many supply houses maintain a staff of trained personnel who can offer helpful advice on any materials. This help is available for the asking. These people are constantly carrying on research to bring new and better material into the field, and are anxious to have teacher reactions.

It is a better rule to overestimate the need than to estimate short on supplies. Anything left over goes into inventory and will reduce the amount to be ordered for the next season. It is sometimes annoying to the school purchasing agent to have to place small fill-in orders during the year. These small orders not only are extra work and perhaps upset the budget, but higher prices are always in order for small purchases. In conclusion, it is just good sense—or politics—to adjust your program to the inventory on hand when first taking a teaching assignment where the materials were ordered by someone else. By developing worth-while projects which call for the use of material that shows a heavy inventory, you will get a balanced stock more quickly and also endear yourself to the "guardians of the purse strings" for the school district.

In purchasing supplies it is usually advantageous—and cheaper—to get a bid on the complete order from several houses and purchase all supplies from one of these.

Some articles are sold at a much lower price when purchased in packages of a definite number of units. Often a total of six units, for instance, in a package is as cheap as five units in a "broken" package. Sometimes this extra unit may be substituted for similar material needed.

Check the price of various-sized papers and cutting costs. Often it is as inexpensive to purchase the larger size and cut to the smaller size, and have the leftover for use. It is also true that double size paper often can be purchased and cut by the teacher at a saving. If a large press-type paper cutter is available in the school, this cutting can be done with ease.

It will be found that providing better brushes—and caring for them—will reduce the cost of brushes and will provide better tools for student work. Many teachers make the mistake of buying cheap brushes. Satisfactory expression cannot be accomplished with inferior tools.

Art supply orders usually become highly individualized. The following list of items are generally needed to carry out the type of program suggested in this book. Other items may be added to or deleted from the list. Several copies of this list may be multigraphed to be used in making out orders, inventories, supply check lists, and for indexing supplies.

163

Tools
air brush
bench hooks
brace and bits
compasses, ink and pencil
chisels
C clamps
drill, egg beater
easels
files
galvanized garbage can
glass cutter
hammers
knives, sloyd
knife, mat
looms
mallet
paper cutter
pliers, round nose
pliers, square nose
punch
rasps
rulers
saws, back, coping, crosscut,
    rip, hack, jewelers
scissors
screw driver
shears, metal
spray gun
stapler
T-squares
tape dispenser
triangles
wire cutters
yard stick

Paints
alcohol
casein
enamel
linseed oil
oil
shellac
silk screen
tempera
textile

turpentine
varnish
watercolor boxes
watercolors, tubes or cakes

Brushes
easel
lettering, flat
lettering, round
oil
stencil
varnish
watercolor

Chalk, Charcoal & Crayon
chalk, board, assorted colors
chalk, lecturer
charcoal, pressed
charcoal, stick
charcoal, stumps
charcoal, erasers
crayons

Pencils
carpenters
charcoal
colored, drawing
graphite, 2H, HB, 2B, 4B, 6B
lithograph

Pens
chisel tip, assorted sizes
drawing
round tip, assorted sizes
ruling

Block Printing Supplies
brayer
cutter sets
gasoline
gasoline dispenser
glass
inks (water or oil)
linoleum

Silk Screen Supplies
adhering liquid
frame

164

film
kerosene
lacquers
liquid glue
organdy
silk
stencil knives
squeegee
turpentine
tusche

Paper
bogus
bristol board
charcoal, white
charcoal, gray
construction, colored
crepe corrugated board
drawing, white
drawing, manila
egg shell mat
illustration board
mimeo
news print
oak tag
poster, assorted colors
project roll
scratch board
water color

Wood & Plastics
ambroid cement
bolts
casein glue
dowels
nails
plastic rods
plastic sheets
sandpaper
screws
wood, balsa
wood, bass
wood, ply
wood, white pine

Clay Materials
clay, moist or powdered

glazes
plaster of Paris
plasticene

Clay Tools
kiln
modelling tools
plaster bats
potters wheel
sponges

Metal
aluminum
asphaltum
copper
emery cloth
etching acid
iron rods
lacquer
pewter
rivets
rouge
screen
sculpt-metal
solder
steel wool
turpentine
wire, aluminum, copper, iron

Metal Tools
blow torch
center punch
drills, assorted
files
forming jigs
hammers, ball pein, planishing
hand drill
mallets, wood, horn, rawhide,
    plastic
polishing wheel
rivet set
sand bags
saws, hack, jewelers
soldering iron

Adhesives
cement, duco
cement, rubber

165

cement, rubber thinner
paste, library
paste, wall paper
tape, cellophane
tape, masking
tape, paper

Miscellaneous
cork
erasers

ink, black and colors
paper clips
paraffin
plaster of Paris
pins, glass push
staples
thread, nylon, sewing and warp
thumbtacks
wire, picture
yarns, weaving

The materials ordered through regular channels can be greatly supplemented by scrap materials which can be located in every community. Local merchants, artisans, and manufacturers are usually willing to co-operate by supplying the schools with leftover, scrap, or spoiled materials. Students can gather many usable items if they are alerted by an enterprising teacher. Arrange some drawers for the storing of such material and carefully sort, index, and neatly store items which may be used. Do not let this area become a junk box where nothing which is needed can ever be located. Here is a list of materials, some of which can be found in most communities:

acetate	containers	leather scraps	ribbons
aluminum foil	copper sheets	linoleum	rope
beads	copper foil	masonite	rug yarn
belts	cord	metal foil	sandpaper
bottles	corn husks	milk containers	sea shells
boxes	costume jewelry	mirrors	sealing wax
burlap	driftwood	muslin	seed pods
buttons	felt	orange sticks	sheepskin
cactus	felt hats	pans	soap
candles	fire extinguishers	paper bags	sponges
canvas	flannel	paper boxes	spools
cartons	floor coverings	paper plates	stockings
celluloid	gimp	paper tubes	stones
cellophane	glass	pine cones	tiles
celotex	gourds	pine needles	tin cans
chains	hat boxes	pipe cleaners	tin foil
chamois	inner tubes	plastics	tongue depressors
clay	jewelry	pocketbooks	twine
cloth	lamp shades	reeds	wallboard

A variety of scrap materials were pleasantly arranged to create this mask.

wallpaper	wooden beads	wooden crates
wax	wooden blocks	wooden dowels
wire	wooden clothespins	yarns
wire screen		

See source book listed at the end of this chapter.

Some PTA groups have taken on the project of collecting scrap materials for the art program.

General school supplies often are the same as materials used in the art program. Prudent use of this supply makes it possible to have available more money in the art budget for the purchase of materials which are uniquely art supplies. Some of these general school supplies are string, thumbtacks, mimeo paper, rulers, pencils, erasers, ink pens, pen holders, library paste, rubber cement, masking tape, cellophane tape, colored paper, crepe paper, blotters, and rubber bands.

The budget

The preparation of the budget in any school system is an extensive job which is very important to all administrators. It must be done well in advance of the school year for which it provides. The art budget, to be included in the general budget, must be prepared in advance. The art teacher will do well to familiarize himself thoroughly with budget procedures and to be as businesslike as possible in his attitude toward them. Here many art teachers appear to be inadequate.

(1) Find out if there is a standard order form used by the school. (2) Determine the amount that the budget provides for art supplies. (3) Procure a copy of last year's order. (4) Find out if there is to be any increase in the school enrollment. For example, if there is to be a ten per cent increase, it is logical to expect a corresponding increase in the art budget. (5) Procure or make an inventory of materials on hand. (6) If the course of study for the next year is to be different from the last, some changes will have to be made accordingly in the amounts and kinds of materials. List these changes.

Before beginning to make out the art supply order, know such things as the deadline date for the budget; amount available for art supplies; provisions made for additional equipment, repairs, and replacements; and any other pertinent factors. Avoid the disappointment of making out a complete order only to find that it does not fit into the over-all school budget, or that it is too late. It is always more satisfactory to adjust one's own order than to have it done by an administrator, when it is discovered that cutting or substitution must be done.

If possible, include an *emergency fund* in the art budget,

168

to care for the purchase of incidental materials as the year progresses.

The amount of money per pupil spent on art supplies varies with the resources of the community, the emphasis on art education, the philosophy of the school, and the breadth of the art program. While attempts are made at running an art program on a very small budget, the most effective and successful programs in the larger junior high schools in this country provide a minimum amount of $6.00 per pupil for art supplies.

The art budget should provide for materials needed; costs of exhibitions; field trips; expansion of activities; changes of enrollment; replacement of old equipment and purchase of new; conference expenses for art personnel; and purchase or rental of audio-visual material and equipment.

Replacement of old and purchase of new equipment usually requires systematic planning which spreads the procurement over several years. As the year progresses, the need for additional quantities or other materials should be noted on a list which can be referred to in making up the next annual order.

Orders should be submitted to bid early in the spring to insure delivery of supplies well before school opens, when several days are required to unpack, check, and store supplies.

Facilities

The nation-wide school building program increases the opportunities for more art teachers to plan their rooms and facilities for their own art curriculum. Each teacher should have such plans well in mind, in case a building program is undertaken in his locality, or he finds an opening elsewhere.

In many instances the present facilities can be used more effectively and supplemented by intelligent, creative planning. Specialized work areas, cabinets, exhibit areas, and other needs can be gradually built into present facilities if an over-all plan is developed and followed.

Location

The art studio should be located on the ground floor

169

and, if possible, near the front entrance to the building. This facilitates the delivery of heavy supplies and exhibition materials. Also exhibits for the education of the entire student body are more readily seen in this location.

The proximity of the art studio to the industrial art shops and the household science departments makes for better integration of these areas.

Space

Because of the variety of activities, equipment, necessary storage space, etc. the art studio must be considerably larger than the average academic classroom, for the same number of pupils. Acoustical treatment is essential because noise accompanies art activities.

Electrical facilities

Adequate lighting facilities should be provided to insure proper amount of simulated daylight to carry on accurate color work on dark days and during evening classes. A northern exposure is preferred as this reduces the changing of the direction of light sources as the sun moves. Additional elec-

A corner of a junior-senior high school room which provides for a number of activities.

PITTSBURGH PUBLIC SCHOOLS, PITTSBURGH, PA.

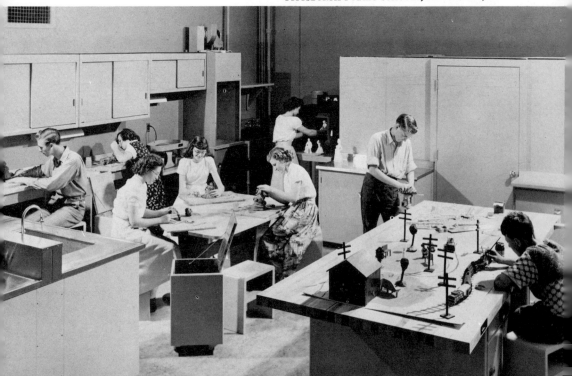

ALL-PURPOSE   **ART WORKSHOP**

ART HORSES

ADEQUATE WALL WORK SPACE

CASES

TACKBOARD

CASES

HORSES OR EASELS

DISPLAY CASES

TACKBOARD

DESK

BOOKS

VISUAL EDUCATION DEMONSTRATIONS

ALL-PURPOSE TABLES

WORK COUNTER STORAGE BELOW

USABLE WORK COUNTER

STUDENT TABLES

SINKS

CASES

ADEQUATE SINK FACILITIES

WHEEL CLAYWORKING AREA

BENCH

HOOD

KILN

SHELVES

RESERVE SUPPLIES

TOOL CASE

SHELVES

CLAYWORKING

STUDENT STORAGE

STUDENT STORAGE

WOODCRAFT BENCH

1 2 3 4 5
SCALE

SHELVES

METALCRAFT BENCH

METALCRAFT

WOODCRAFT

This plan occupies the space of one and a half ordinary classrooms. The space is 48' x 22'.

E. H. SHELDON EQUIPMENT COMPANY

trical outlets are necessary along the walls for saws, power tools, airbrush, spotlights, miniature stages, three-dimensional displays, and projection equipment. A pull-down projection screen should be mounted directly above the chalkboard. A 220 volt cable is usually required for electric kilns. Power tools and kilns should have separate lines with a panel box which can be locked.

Gas inlets

Several gas inlets are needed for metalwork and jewelry. If a gas-fired kiln is used, a master valve should be provided.

Storage

Very few art rooms have enough storage space. If three-dimensional art work is carried on as encouraged in this book, a considerable amount of storage space is needed for work in progress as well as for completed creations. All paper and cardboard must be stored flat. Shallow drawers on rollers are ideal for this.

If the yearly supplies are stored in the art rooms, considerable space has to be provided. *Tools* can be stored on portable panels so that they can easily be moved to various work areas in the room. Vertical racks on cabinet tops will provide storage space for *oil paintings* and unfinished *charcoal* and *pastel drawings*.

Individual lock cabinets will provide for storage of expensive personal materials, brushes, jewelry, leathercraft, etc.

Water

Plenty of sink space will reduce clean-up time. Sinks which project into the room will provide space for pupils on two or three sides at the same time. Wall areas near the sink should be covered with some waterproof material which can easily be kept clean. Clay and grease traps must be installed to prevent clogging of drain pipes.

Exhibition space

Provide as much exhibit space as possible. Cabinet doors will serve for tacking up flat materials. Tops of low cabinets,

172

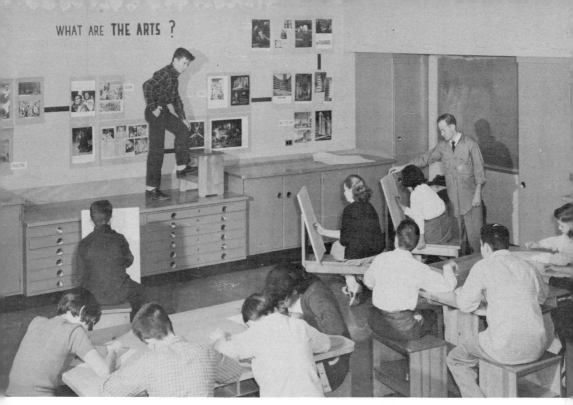

A junior high school figure sketching class with a student model.

shelves, and stands can serve as display space for three-dimensional work. Walls can be covered with cork or inexpensive "celotex" for exhibiting flat work. Pine panelling is also very practical, as it is soft, holds tacks, and doesn't show tack marks too badly.

Glass display cases built into the walls which separate the art studio from the corridor facilitates setting up displays for student viewing. Glass shelves can provide for the display of three-dimensional work.

Alternate facilities

Lack of facilities will not present an unsurmountable obstacle for the creative art teacher. Just as there are many scrap materials which can be used in building an art program, there are. many ways to overcome the lack of space for art classes. One art teacher, without an art studio for student use, actually transformed an old coal bin into a satisfactory room when the heaters were converted to gas from

173

coal. Adequate lighting made this into a generous-sized and practical art studio. Often large corridors have been utilized for a sketch class or to carry on work on large murals or stage sets. Unused ends of corridors often can be walled and converted into work rooms. The cafeteria can double as an art room if storage space and necessary facilities are provided. In small schools industrial arts shops have been successfully combined with the art studio. Some of the more successful larger schools have developed this ideal situation. The range of art productions which can be developed in this type of combination is almost unlimited. Some small schools have combined the art and music studios.

Anyway, as has been previously pointed out, the most important element in the successful art program is the creative art teacher!

Reference
Grice, George, representative for J. L. Hammett Co., Lyons, N. Y.

Teacher Reference
Sources of Free and Inexpensive Educational Materials, Field Enterprises, Inc., Educational Division, Merchandise Mart Plaza, Chicago 54, Ill., 1955.

Alphabetized subject index and directory of sources of many free and inexpensive materials and teaching aids.

CHAPTER X　　　　　　　PUBLIC RELATIONS

To BE most effective, the art program—in addition to providing a vital, interesting, and exciting series of activities—needs the support of the school administration and staff, the parents, the student body, and the general public. In order to gain and maintain support from these groups, they must be kept aware of the art program. This calls for an organized plan to provide information making full use of all resources.

Furthermore, the whole program of general education needs public support. Art—like music, dramatics, industrial arts, and physical education—has the inherent qualities for providing a considerable amount of favorable public relations. Therefore the art department is obligated to promote the cause of general education.

An interesting story is told about the businessman's approach to this problem of constant promotion. An executive group of the Wrigley Company were traveling by train to a company conference. Mr. Phil Wrigley began talking about a million-dollar advertising campaign. One of his executives said, "Why should we spend that much money on advertising? Already we are selling all the gum that we can make and nearly everyone in America now chews gum." Wrigley is reported to have asked, "How fast do you think this train is going?" Some one suggested about 70 mph. "Well," said Wrigley, "then if everything is running smoothly and we are going as fast as necessary, why not detach the engine?" So it is with an art program. Even the best on-going program needs to maintain its pace by keeping public support.

*A puppet show involves many art problems and a sense of
cooperative dramatics.*

Student interest

Probably the best way to promote the art program is
through student contact. All of the youngsters can be good-
will ambassadors. If they are excited about their work, their
enthusiasm will carry over to the rest of the student body, to
the staff, and to the parents.

Most individuals enjoy publicity. See that interesting and unusual art activities are publicized in school and local papers. Arrange regular exhibits so that art students have a chance to show off their accomplishments to their schoolmates.

If art is being taught as an *elective course,* arrange to have other students audit the art classes. This has been done in some schools by having descriptive announcements made of art projects before they begin. Then students who might like to work on any of these have been invited to come from study halls for the period of time that this project continues. This has caused many students to register for an art course the following semester or to join an art club in order to carry on art activities with more regularity.

Art clubs also provide for those students who want to carry on work in specialized areas when such work might not be practical in a regular classroom situation. Art clubs can be organized to study films, periods of art, jewelry making, crafts, and other specialties. Also club members might plan and arrange for all exhibitions. Some art clubs handle the school advertising programs.

Adolescents' interest in art can be maintained through projects and materials which challenge their skills.

MAMARONECK JUNIOR HIGH SCHOOL, MAMARONECK, N. Y.

Projects in social studies classes often are the stimulus for correlated art problems. Through such activities, adolescent interest in art is often maintained for many students.

Students derive considerable satisfaction from the reaction of parents when their work is displayed for P.T.A. meetings, open house, or parents' night.

Well planned field trips also generate interest in the art courses.

Often parents seek advice as to what they can do to sustain the interest of a child in art. Parents can be encouraged to provide art materials, home studios, trips to exhibitions and galleries, and, when advisable, to enroll the child in Saturday-morning classes.

In some large city schools, students are released during school hours to take credit courses in local museums with professional artists as instructors. Smaller schools have successfully engaged local artists and craftsmen to come to art classes

178

once a week to work with the art teacher on some specialty such as jewelry, ceramics, stone carving, weaving, etc.

Advertising flyers can be used to advantage to describe courses, sequences, vocational opportunities, avocational outcomes, and other pertinent information for students and parents. These can be mimeographed forms, or, as is done in some city schools, well-designed and printed pieces of advertising art in several colors.

Of course slides, strip films, and action films make for a more interesting art course for students and provide material for talks to adult groups. These should never be used, however, until previewed and thoroughly analyzed by the instructor. They should not be used as time fillers. When outstanding films are available, which are of general interest to all students, art assemblies can be arranged, or they can be shown during lunch periods. Also students can be invited from study halls when films are shown during regular class hours. Many art films are of interest to students in social-studies classes.

Staff support

The support of the school staff is an important factor in developing interest in an art program. In order to develop this support, the art teacher must show a genuine interest in the work of other staff members. The art teacher must be alert to the aims and problems of other departments. He cannot isolate himself within the art area.

Being conversant with trends and practices in general education will enable the art teacher to place proper emphasis on art in the over-all program. Only with this background can worth-while contributions be made to staff discussions.

It is likely that many of the promotional ideas suggested in this chapter which are aimed at creating interest in other groups will also serve to stimulate art interest and understanding among the staff.

Teachers will appreciate the help of the art teacher in arranging classroom displays. Ofttimes effective mounting papers and illustrative materials can be provided. Whenever possible, integrate art with the classroom work of other de-

179

partments. Generally academic teachers will welcome lectures or demonstrations to classes by the art teacher when it can make a valuable contribution to the subject at hand.

Staff-member hobby shows often prove interesting when held in connection with faculty meetings.

One of the most effective means of gaining staff interest is to involve teachers in the creative art process through staff workshops.

Administration support

More often than not school administrators begin a conversation about art education by saying, "I really don't know anything about art." This is often due to lack of background in art education and, incidentally, to the fact that art teachers have been delinquent in providing information.

One school administrator observed at a state art association meeting that "Superintendents are besieged, not sold, by various departments." Most superintendents are ready to support any subject area when it is "sold" or proved to be of value. If the teachers in a particular area do not make it important, and prove its worth, it will continue to lack support.

Conducting a program of art in which students and parents are interested is the most obvious and best possible way of gaining administration support.

Administrators are busy with the general problems of education. They do not have time to seek out current articles or reports on specific areas. When art teachers find significant information which will help to develop an understanding of art education, they should underline this, or make a short resume of it, and forward it to the administration. Easily read reports concerning the activities and plans of the art department should be regularly prepared and sent to the administration. Include reports on students who have been helped to adjust to school life through art activities. See that accomplishments of former art students are published in the school and town paper, or otherwise come to the attention of the administration.

Let the administration know of any art programs, such as marionette shows, slide talks, or technical demonstrations, for community organizations.

180

A workshop for classroom teachers conducted by the author. Emphasis is on designing projects with scrap materials.

The art teacher should be willing to speak to local groups, and to represent the school on any occasion.

Scheduling

Be ever alert to the most effective ways possible for scheduling art classes, and submit schedule ideas to those responsible for the over-all program.

As many adolescent art programs call for only two or three class periods a week, they often have to be integrated with similar schedules in other courses. If the school policy fortunately calls for art classes to meet daily throughout the year, then the scheduling is made very simple. If, however, classes meet only a few times a week, or daily for a period of several weeks, the scheduling is more complicated.

Some schools have worked out an effective schedule by having art classes meet two periods per week and music classes two periods, and a combined art and music assembly one day, to complete the five-day week.

In some instances, art is scheduled for five days per week for a period of time such as twelve or eighteen weeks. Then the students move on to some other class, such as music or industrial arts, for an equal time.

Advantages of this are:

1. The number of different pupils per teacher per week is greatly reduced.

2. The teacher gets to know the pupils better, in a more concentrated program.

3. Guidance is more effective because of this.

4. Student interest is better focused on the course.

However, some teachers prefer to have classes meet two or three times a week so that contact can be maintained throughout the year.

Some schools arrange separate art classes for boys and girls. In this situation, usually the boys go to physical education while the girls go to art and vice versa.

Advantages of this are:

1. Activities which have greater appeal and meaning to boys or girls are selected by each group. These activities are often very different.

2. Having similar types of work underway in a class enable an instructor to be of greater help to more people.

3. Smaller classes.

4. Lack of self-consciousness makes for more naturalness and sincerity—less "playing to the gallery."

The greatest disadvantage of this plan is that it fails to provide for the social mingling of the sexes which is such an important part of art activities for early adolescents.

Public promotion

A variety of means is available for providing information concerning the art program to parents and the general pub-

182

lic. Dramatize your story, using every available medium—newspapers, radio, television, window displays, films, lectures, demonstrations, flyers, community art groups, P.T.A.'s., exhibitions, hobby shows, adult art classes, Halloween decorations, letters to parents, and conferences.

Newspapers. Most schools will be able to use newspapers more than any other outside medium.

Novices at publicity will do well to cultivate the acquaintance of reporters and obtain their advice. Study as many newspapers as possible in order to develop a journalistic slant on news articles. (Teachers in large schools will probably have the assistance of a school public-relations director.)

A well-written article for a small newspaper is often printed as presented. Style may not be so important for the larger paper, for a member of its own staff may rewrite all copy. Find out the procedure.

Deliver news to the paper promptly. Twenty-four-hour-old news is stale for a daily paper. Know what the deadlines are and be prompt. Even important news cannot be printed if it arrives after the deadline.

If there is more than one newspaper in a community, there is bound to be rivalry. Give each one an even break. If an afternoon paper gets a release one time, be sure that the morning paper gets the next release.

All news stories must tell who, what, when and where. The first paragraph should give this information in a brief resume of the article. Be 100 per cent sure of spelling, dates, and time. Avoid flowery language, slang, and professional jargon. Tell your story briefly but fully in simple language with reasonably short sentences and paragraphs.

1. All material should be typed.

2. A release date should be placed in the upper lefthand corner with the name, address, and phone number of the person offering the information.

3. Copy should be double or triple spaced on one side of the paper only.

4. Begin article half or two-thirds of the way down the first page, which provides room for a copy editor to type head-

183

ings or to rewrite the lead. Leave ample margins on both sides.

5. Number all pages.

6. At the bottom of each page, except the last, type the word "more" to indicate unfinished copy.

7. Mark the end of the article by the word "end" or by the symbol "30" or "###."

Be alert for newspaper picture possibilities. Strongly contrasting, glossy prints are necessary, if you can provide the photos. Candid or action shots are most popular.

Papers usually prefer staff photographs.

Radio and television. These two media have steadily become more popular and important in publicizing school activities. While radio does not lend itself so well to portraying the work of the art program, television is a natural for showing either activities or the finished product from art classes. Radio, however, can more readily dramatize some stories, and, of course, the radio news broadcasts are effective means of reaching the public with information concerning art activities. Remember that radio and television news programs are competitors with newspapers. Give them equal opportunities to handle news releases.

Many conversational-type radio programs can readily build a broadcast around an interesting art project, a new medium, interior decoration problems, or an exhibition. Whenever you feel you might have an interesting possibility for a program, write it up briefly, and the radio program director will decide on its merits.

The art teacher will need more than a "good idea" and a dramatic sense to produce an effective television show. Seek the advice of experts if a TV show is to be presented. A poorly presented show can be worse than no show at all. Larger schools may have one person in charge of this area, who is familiar with broadcasting problems and techniques. Teachers in small schools will need the assistance of station experts.

There are as yet many unexplored possibilities in using television for education. One large school system uses TV shows to inform the art staff in the city schools of the new developments, new media, techniques, and plans. One uni-

184

A master craftswoman brought into the classroom to exhibit her creations, lecture on a little-known craft, and to demonstrate spinning and weaving. Her assistant is her granddaughter, a junior high student, demonstrating the process of carding wool preparatory to spinning.

versity is now offering an extension course for credit by TV. The professor in charge lectures and demonstrates from the station while assistants occasionally meet with groups who are taking the course.

185

Ninth grade boys demonstrate the completion of their wood carvings.

Exhibits. Art exhibits bring culture to the community, provide opportunities for understanding and evaluating the art program, bring parents to the school, stimulate student interest, and promote education generally.

If an exhibition gallery is available in the school, it should be constantly used to show interesting material of some kind. The gallery is an ideal means of integrating art with various areas of the curriculum and with industrial or community life.

Many spaces can provide an exhibition area — unused chalkboards, corridors, cafeterias, libraries, gymnasiums, public buildings, lobbies, store windows. Bulletin boards and folding screens may be used for flat display. Three-dimensional displays may be shown on library tables, cafeteria tables, book cases, display cases, or boxes, and, of course, many articles can be suspended for effective display.

Choose an area which can be readily lighted, with reasonable provision for circulation of people, and where the work can be shown to advantage.

The exhibit itself should be a work of art—well organized and not overcrowded. The posters, direction signs, identification cards, and catalogues should all be well designed with, some given theme and color scheme running throughout. The number of pieces shown can easily be limited when non-student work is exhibited. Sometimes the student shows demand that more work be displayed than can be gracefully fitted into the exhibition space. In such a situation the most effective pieces can be displayed in the main gallery, and additional pieces of two-dimensional work can be arranged in folios for those who care to look. Excessive three-dimensional projects can be displayed in adjoining rooms or in corridors.

Use a variety of materials as backgrounds, to unify the show, or to emphasize areas. Examples: burlap, cork, pegboard, monks cloth, cardboard, corrugated paper, ropes, yarn, wire screens, metal lath, and "celotex."

Exhibits of current work can be continuously shown throughout the year. Exhibits can be correlated with special events such as holidays, dances, ball games, P.T.A. meetings, festivals, and open house.

An extensive, well-planned, annual show of the student work of the whole year should be given. This will interest the students, parents, and general public. This annual art show can be built up into a most important function of the school year. The art club or art classes will benefit from the organizational work of preparing news releases, posters, invitations, and catalogues, and from hanging the show and acting as guides.

Small art displays can be effectively set up in store windows, public libraries, bank lobbies, and other public buildings. In arranging store window displays, be sure to contact the store manager for his ideas on display techniques. Do not be too *avante garde* with public exhibitions. The produc-

187

Book marks made by seventh grade students as gifts for visiting sixth-grade students who come during the orientation period. These could also be used for open house or parents' night.

tions shown must not be too far beyond what the audience expects or can understand. Shocking the public is not the best method of enlisting its support.

Interesting exhibits can be obtained from local artists, summer resident artists, state and federal agencies, teachers colleges, art education associations, universities, private collectors, commercial and industrial agencies, museums, clubs, guilds, and craftsmen.

188

Hobby and home craft shows will arouse interest and indicate to local people that you are interested in their efforts. Also exhibits of this kind bring into the schools people who might not be inclined to come for a pure, fine art show.

An exhibition must be planned in a businesslike manner. Don't approach an artist or a collector with a request for his works unless you have a definite plan in mind. Explain how and where the works are to be shown. Plan and indicate a safe method of transporting the works. Be prepared to insure the exhibit while being transported and shown. *Arrange for protection* while the works are on exhibition. Remember that most art pieces cannot be replaced. Be sure to check with individual artists regarding copy to be used for publicity. Artists will appreciate the publicity, as this serves as a partial return for their efforts.

Other ideas on promoting public relations

1. Adult art classes. This brings many persons into the school to become active supporters of your program.

Making the book marks.

ROCKY MOUNT CITY SCHOOLS, ROCKY MOUNT, N. C.

2. Teas for parents of art students. These occasions enable the art teacher to meet many parents and to explain what is being attempted in art education.

3. Holiday decorations. Store window decorations for Halloween will prove a successful means of showing student art to most of the community. By means of large community Christmas displays, the art classes can help to create a holiday atmosphere.

4. Lectures and demonstrations. Most civic groups will welcome an apt talk or demonstration related to art. These provide an interested audience to which an explanation of the art philosophy of the school can be directed.

5. P.T.A. groups have a special interest in everything going on in the schools. Contact them for support of the art program.

6. Community art groups. These groups include those who are generally interested in art in addition to those who feel they are able to create. Be active in these groups. If none exists in your community, use your influence and prestige to organize one.

Be animated about your own program and spread the doctrine of art education wherever you are. Your enthusiasm will be contagious!

CHAPTER XI EVALUATION

PROBABLY no other specific area in the whole educational structure presents more of a problem for the art teacher than that of evaluation. Yet it is a most important factor and one with which we all have to contend.

Many art educators feel that a grade should not be given in art. However, students and parents have come to expect grades for all school activities. If we do not grade the art course, we risk the possibility of art being considered as of less importance than the academics which appear to be more readily measured. In some cases even letter grades such as A, B, and C will not be accepted. Numerical grades are demanded.

Perhaps the ideal manner of conveying to parents the progress of their children is through regularly scheduled personal conferences, despite the risk attached. Too often a conference means that there are serious problems to be discussed. Another drawback is that individual parent-teacher conferences on grades take more time than the average teacher has available. Also concise grades of a number or letter are being demanded for office records, guidance counseling, report cards, college credentials, employment services, etc. Therefore we must be realistic about evaluation, which is to give the most meaningful grade possible for each pupil in the art course.

The problem then is what to look for in establishing a grade, and what does the grade represent. Can a mathe-

191

matical grade serve as a meaningful report of human development? Can creativity be arranged on an evaluation scale? Do we evaluate accomplishment or effort? Do we evaluate the person, the process, the product—or all three?

In the more traditional type of art teaching, grading was a comparatively simple matter. Art consisted mostly of making drawings of objects which appeared as similar to the models as the students could make them. The highest grade went to the pupil who made the best reproduction on paper. Design grades were based on the best technical rendition. Creativity, personal expression, and originality, if recognized, were not stressed. Grades were determined with considerable accuracy. Everyone knew what the grade meant. Charles with a 90 in art had talent and could draw a little more realistically than Mary who earned an 88% grade.

Valid grades are not so easily determined in our broader concept of art education. Evaluation requires an intimate understanding of the pupil, the process, and the product.

The *product* is a physical representation of the creative process and the personality expressed. In the product we look not merely at an end result—a work of art. The product represents to us much more than a detached, abstract organization of materials and design principles. The product represents orginality, creativity, selection, and adaptation of materials and technical skills. The sincerity and satisfaction of the student expression as seen through the finished product is what gives it meaning to us as educators.

Only a very general scale can be devised for evaluating creative products, as creativity itself is such a uniquely personal and individual affair. The product isolated by itself is of little or no worth in evaluation. The *process* and the product are organically intertwined. So our evaluation must be given in terms of what we know from having watched the creativity from its inception through completion. The creative process is not only an indication of growth but also an instrument of growth.

In order to make a valid evaluation of the product and process we must know the creator—the person, or pupil. This means, of necessity, that evaluation is not something which

192

takes place only at the end of the semester or a work unit. Much of our evaluation must begin when we initiate our contact with the student.

It seems unfair to fail students who do not finally measure up to a pre-determined, dead-level end standard unless we can begin with students who are all equal. We know that this is impossible. Each student is an individual with personal powers and weaknesses. It is essential that we know as much as possible about the attitudes and abilities of all students at the beginning of our association with them. Then we must grade partly on their growth and development as individuals, and partly on their productions.

As we discussed earlier in this book, there is a tremendous spread in the developmental stages of early maturation. The grade must be determined by where the student is in relation to where his starting position was. The teacher must familiarize himself with the student through personal contacts, cumulative records, a variety of projects, and conferences with parents and former teachers.

There are available means of measuring intelligence with reasonable accuracy. Creative ability can be recognized rather easily. The ability to stick to a problem—personal drive—is much harder to measure. We know that this ability varies in degrees as do all other traits. If a student lacks this quality—which is necessary in creativity—should he be penalized for the lack? Our evaluation must be based upon the degree of development which takes place in terms of the personal potentialities of each individual pupil.

In evaluation of the *pupil, process,* and *product* it must be determined if—

1. Evidence of originality, knowledge, appreciation, and judgment grows in proper proportion to technical skills, and in well-chosen avenues of expression.

2. There is development in the ability to stay with a project—to see it through.

3. Resolution, purpose, and accomplishment are achieved rather than confusion and misapplication of powers.

4. Individual development is taking place rather than mere participation in "busy work."

193

5. Past experiences are being integrated into the solution of problems.

6. The approach is one of interpretation rather than imitation.

7. Aesthetic sensitivity is being developed along with self-confidence.

8. Respect is gained for personal abilities, materials, tools, and the rights of others.

Our evaluation is carried on in the light of our aims. We want the student to develop creativity and originality. In addition to encouraging this self-expression, we want him to discover what is important to him about art, to develop appreciation and understanding. We hope that he emerges a better integrated personality, with increased strength for the completion of more difficult tasks.

"The educational value of a procedure used with any child can be measured to a great degree by the evidences of changing power in the child to stand by his task to completion, by his ability to be self-critical to the end, and by his desire constantly to raise the self-imposed standard of accomplishment at the end of each production."[1]

The students should live up to their own standards. Each youth should be encouraged to work to the peak of his ability. Continued interest is usually contingent upon satisfaction resulting from giving one's best.

Though the production of works of art is not the aim, no student benefits from meaningless and carelessly executed work. Constructive leadership calls for a definite plan for continuous evaluation and program development. Otherwise, the art course becomes a series of unguided, time-consuming projects which cannot be justified in the light of our aims.

Occasionally every teacher discovers unusual talent which augurs well for success in the art world. These students should be encouraged. The art teacher can make a significant contribution to society by discovering and encouraging talented young people. It is good for the soul of an art teacher to find fresh, powerful work which can be justifiably praised and enjoyed for its singular merits.

Most early adolescents are easily discouraged. They are

194

very sensitive to criticism. Their interest in creativity wavers and can easily disappear, to be replaced by other fleeting interests in which they find temporary security. Evaluation alone must never be so contrived that it causes the student to lose faith in creative investigation, thought and expression.

The development of a desire for technical proficiency grows as the student matures and is motivated by the urge for better self-expression in areas in which he is most interested. Evaluation helps to determine these interests and to keep a check on developmental stages.

Be alert to the great spread of emotional and physical maturity in the junior high students. A creation which may be meaningful to one student may be meaningless to another. If a rigid standard of measurement is set up for all students, the weaker and less mature students will not be able to meet them, through no fault of their own, and this will result in discouragement and destruction of any confidence they may have had. This of course, is diametrically opposed to what we are attempting to accomplish in art education on this level.

Evaluation of the student's work serves to determine the extent of the particular student's growth, enabling us to more effectively motivate and guide the student in his creative efforts, aesthetic understanding and personality development.

Evaluation is a constant process. From it we determine where our teaching as well as the student's development, has been weak or successful. We learn the extent to which we have come to know and to understand each student, and adjust accordingly.

Reference

MacDonald, Rosabell, *Art as Education,* Henry Holt & Co., New York, 1941, p. 14.

Much

T HE TEACHERS of art are fortunate in that there is such an abundance of available material to aid them. Even without a special department set-up to supply audio-visual aids, they can locate many materials for stimulating interest and the learning processes.

Magazines are source material for studying page layout, design, illustration, typography, lettering, interior decoration, photography, and landscaping. Local buildings can provide for the study of architecture. Nature supplies landscapes and seascapes for painting. Industrial design can be studied through products and packages. Posters supply examples of advertising art. Slides illustrate in almost endless variety every form of art created by man. Books offer a treasure of source material.

Ofttimes effective and available teaching aids are overlooked. Students studying color will be amazed to discover that they carry on their finger nails a whole gamut of color. (Have them hold up their thumbnail to the sunlight or a strong electric light and look at it very closely. They will find that there are hundreds of small particles of rainbow colors.)

The textures and forms found in natural and manmade objects serve as inspirations in creating compositions. Many students who feel that they are not aesthetically sensitive will be inclined to reconsider when they are made conscious of their own reaction to a glorious sunset or sunrise, to a ridge of hills at dusk, to the graceful lines of a suspension bridge, to the silhouette of a city skyline, to the impressive dignity of a giant seguaro cactus, or to "amber waves of grain." Have students collect various materials to discover the many textures available. Use sunlight to study form as indicated by light and shade; point out how shadows from a warm light source are cool in color; demonstrate the principle of reflected light. Use corridors and streets to demonstrate perspective. In creative projects make use of natural and scrap materials found in every community. When audial, visual, and tactile experiences in our environment are used as stimuli and references, art becomes a more vital part of our everyday living.

Resources

Make use of all available teaching aids. Survey the local community for points of interest, architecture, sculpture, art collections, craft shops, churches, museums, artists, designers, and architects. Know what art objects and reference materials are available in the school and local libraries and museums. Provide as many art magazines, books, and prints as possible for student reference.

If the school has an audio-visual department, procure a list of all art reference material on hand. Determine what the budget provides for rental and purchase of audio-visual aids, and make use of it.

Films can be obtained free from many industrial organizations and foreign government travel bureaus. Lists of available slides and films will be provided by one or more of the following: audio-visual director, principal, state college, state education department, and regional art education associations.

Music. If a record player is used in the art classes, many students will gladly furnish records to be used for mood music or motivation. Appropriate music serves to create interest in the art classes and to provide an atmosphere for creative work.

When radio and television broadcasts concerning art are scheduled, inform all art students and encourage them to tune in. These broadcasts are becoming frequent and worth while.

Slides

At least one school with a very limited budget has as-

197

sembled an outstanding collection of slides of the world's most important paintings. This was done by the art teacher, who made color slides from reproductions in art books and folios. While these are not as perfect as slides made directly from the originals, they do make satisfactory illustrations available for students. Slides made from student work are valuable aids in presenting similar projects to subsequent classes.

Slides are available from many museums at little or no cost. Other sources of slides are state universities, regional art associations, state education departments, industrial organizations, and private photographers.

The Metropolitan Museum of Art in New York has made available an extensive series of small reproductions of great works of art which can be projected for study with opaque projectors.

Films

Many educational films are now available for art classes. Effective use of films in teaching requires advance planning. Some of the most popular films have to be ordered months ahead. This is especially true when a film is needed on a specific date in order to fit into the teaching or projection schedule.

Students should be oriented for each film in order to insure benefits from viewing it. The film should not begin beyond youthful understanding and experience. All films should be previewed by the teacher. If time permits it is often advantageous to review the film with students after it has been seen and evaluated.

Exhibition

Displays of art work should be constantly provided in as many places in the school as is feasible. Practical hints on arranging exhibitions are given in Chapter X.

Exchange exhibits with other schools provide an excellent source for a series of displays. This can be arranged with schools in the same system, neighboring schools, and out-of-state or foreign schools. Usually the only cost for these is the postage involved. Students enjoy seeing work done on their own level by students in other locations.

198

Field trips

Often a field trip to a gallery, museum, studio, or art center can be a more effective teaching aid than any other. Field trips cost money and use a considerable amount of student time, so they should be carefully arranged for in order to derive as much benefit as possible from them. Students should be given adequate background for trips, and a follow-up discussion is essential.

If guides are available at the destination, they are usually worth the cost.

In planning a field trip:

1. Make definite arrangements with officials of the place to be visited.
2. Arrange for student releases from classes.
3. Obtain parental permission when required.
4. Arrange transportation well in advance.
5. Carefully plan the route and financing.
6. Arrange for adequate supervision.
7. Plan for eating arrangements, and rest stops.
8. Discuss clothing and deportment.

Plan field trips, as all other art projects, to make them the most informative, exciting, educational experiences possible.

The intimate association with young people as they thrill to the unfolding of the never ending expanse of art experiences, and the opportunity to be an effective instrument in their growth and development resulting from creative experiences makes art teaching a stimulating and satisfying vocation.

Film Lists

1. *Educational Film Guide,* H. W. Wilson Co., 950 University Ave., New York 52, N. Y.

    All 16 mm. films intended for educational use; all sponsored or "free" films, documentary and experimental films.
2. *Educators Guide to Free Films,* Educators Progress Service, Randolph, Wisconsin.
3. *Films for Classroom Use,* Teaching Films Custodians Inc., 25 West 43rd Street, New York 18, N. Y.
4. *Films for the Study and Enjoyment of Art,* Free booklet from International Film Bureau Inc., 57 E. Jackson Blvd., Chicago 4, Ill.

INDEX